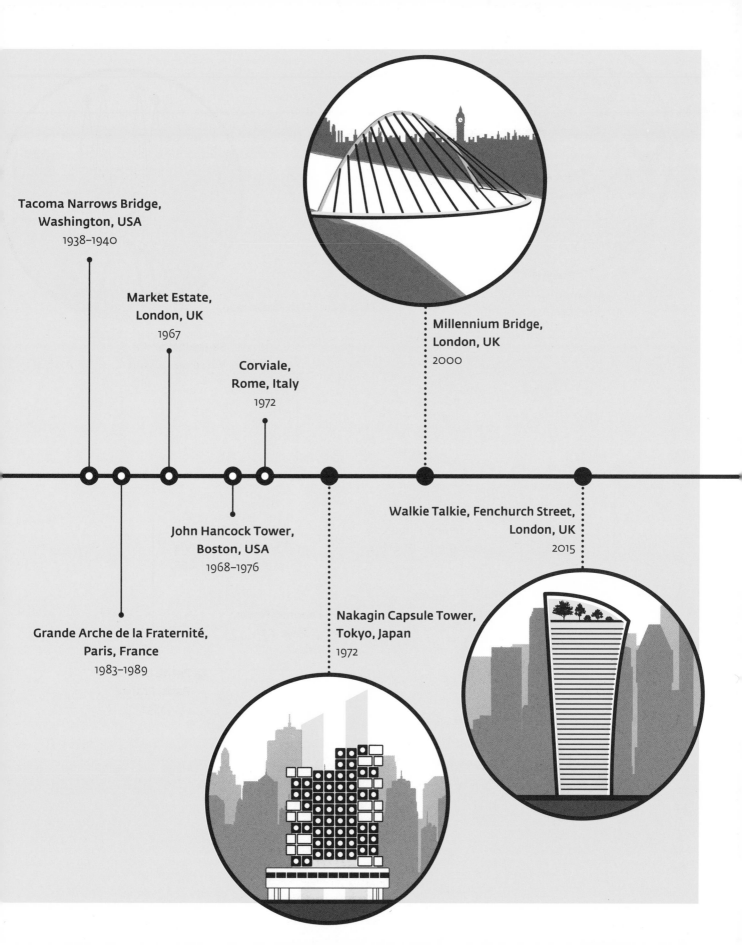

Tacoma Narrows Bridge, Washington, USA
1938–1940

Market Estate, London, UK
1967

Corviale, Rome, Italy
1972

Millennium Bridge, London, UK
2000

John Hancock Tower, Boston, USA
1968–1976

Walkie Talkie, Fenchurch Street, London, UK
2015

Grande Arche de la Fraternité, Paris, France
1983–1989

Nakagin Capsule Tower, Tokyo, Japan
1972

CONTENTS

THE NEW KICK IN THE STOMACH ESTHETIC

Alessandro Biamonti

FAILURE

This book brings together cases of outstanding failures – a fascinating topic with broad implications.

We are living in a moment in history when the concept of failure is being reinterpreted, especially through the search for and proposal of new reasons to conceive it as an opportunity rather than a problem. This involves a profound, wide-ranging reinterpretation that begins on a personal level and expands to the larger ideological questions that have affected – and continue to affect – entire societies and nations.

Every evolution – whether it be technological, philosophical or social – requires that the preceding technology, philosophy or society be surmounted, and thus in effect, that it fails. From this perspective, the history of mankind could be seen as a continual accumulation or stratification of results, techniques and modes of thought that are no longer suitable.

Thus, human history is built over layers of rubble and failures, ruins with which we have always lived. Despite our familiarity with these desolate landscapes, it is still not fully accepted that things, people and modes of thought can become unsuitable at a certain point, and that it is precisely this condition that often serves as the generator of something new. Perhaps this is related to the idea in Darwin's theory of evolution that unfit species die out. The fate of human beings is less cruel, however; not only can they survive failure, but they can be strengthened by it and emerge prepared to face new challenges.

In the definition of this new approach to failure, Steve Jobs' speech in 2005 represents a true milestone that set the direction for an entire new millennium. Addressing the Stanford graduating class, Jobs listed a series of failures and misfortunes, to which, however, he attributed part of the merit for his career and his luck. He concluded with the famed exhortation, "Stay hungry. Stay foolish".

RUINS

For cultures that understand "building" as leaving a mark on history, ruins have always been part of the landscape. So it is throughout Italy. Italians have always been forced to come to terms with the remains of an ancient past. This past, of which we are so proud, becomes part of the background, of the scenery and of our very experience of the contemporary. The "missed present" is something else altogether. In fact, while the ruins of the past are usually given prominence and glorified by constructing a sort of "pedestal" that transforms them into "history lessons", the same cannot be said about contemporary ruins. Here, the tendency is either to destroy or modernize them – in other words, to eliminate them in one way or another – as if to purge all signs of failure from the landscape.

This is because contemporary ruins have something sublime about them, something tender and horrifying at the same time, like old sci-fi films from the 1950s in which the future is envisioned as a world full of tin space ships whose occupants are busily communicating with old-fashioned valve radios. Today, when we watch these videos on our iPhones, or maybe even on the latest wrist device, that obsolete "future" is actually rather endearing.

We experience this same compassion before the "missed present" of those objects that were designed to be something that they are not or that they have never become, and thus appear today as the ruined vestiges of a mode of thought.

Their physical nature as ruins cannot be denied, yet they do not emanate the poetry and beauty that past generations of artists constructed around historical ruins. Here we stand before disarming landscapes that make the blood run cold and have a formidable "kick in the stomach" esthetic. Yet, at the same time, something emerges that fascinates us and makes us stay, drawing us in. In fact, even if we are looking at the graceless remains of discarded construction materials, we are capable of establishing an empathy with them that is impossible with historical ruins. Indeed, despite our elaborate reconstructions, it is difficult to step into the shoes of an ancient Roman and truly experience his daily life, whereas we ourselves are the missing inhabitants of contemporary ruins.

This may be why we find ourselves looking so carefully at those rusty sheets of metal, that unfinished reinforced concrete, those materials that are slowly crumbling – because we represent their missing anthropological component. These ruins do not speak dead ancient languages, buried in the sands of time or known only by a select and cultured few; they speak our language. We are part of the same story because we live on the same page of history.

THE PROJECT

Ettore Sottsass just may be the Italian designer who has left the greatest cultural legacy in the world of design. Surely he is a designer whose reflections have become required knowledge for the international community. In his autobiography, he confessed "I'm a friend of uncertain, baffled, modest people, who try to understand but always feel like those who don't understand. I'm a very close friend of fearful people."

Thus Sottsass exposes his own existential fragility – something new and unexpected from a 20th-century designer insofar as it brings into question the confidence of one whose project or design leaves his mark on history. In fact, in the second half of the last century, something shifted in the design world. A new phenomenon emerged, born of the Modern Movement's loss of self-confidence, which, despite its stated desire to effect a radical break with the past, still possessed a vision of architecture whose deep and irrevocable signs set it in history as a permanent phenomenon.

It is precisely this aspiration to "permanence" – historically a symbol of strength – that in the postmodernity of the last century (and especially of this century) proved somewhat inadequate with respect to the contemporary condition. The Modern Movement planned trustingly for a positive future – an attitude that allowed for no *défaillances*. After World War II, after all the atrocities of that period, the planners – that is, those who took on the task of creating the places of the immediate future – felt that they could not make any mistakes; they felt a responsibility to provide the world with the appropriate conditions to grow and develop again safely. This feeling of security and trust is quite close to the idea of "faith", in the sense of something that cannot and must not be questioned and that is put into practice and celebrated through works, especially the construction of places dedicated to those principles, as was done throughout the centuries by the builders of the great temples and cathedrals.

Thus, the Modern Movement set about creating its own "cathedrals". Much more quickly than the cathedrals of the past, however, these imposing presences showed an unforeseen fragility, inadequacy, need for maintenance, etc. Their unplanned imperfection means that we see them as ruins to be included, albeit tenderly, in our daily lives.

There may be no better expression of this tender fragility of the Modern, though also perhaps of its strength, than images of Le Corbusier's project in Chandigarh as it is today. Building this capital of two states virtually from scratch offered an extraordinary opportunity for Le Corbusier to materialize his philosophy of the city explicitly in architecture.

In fact, he planned the "silver city" as a large urban organism, whose similarities to the human body have often been cited; the parks are the city's "lungs" while the "circulatory system" is the road system in which pedestrian and automobile routes are separated and organized hierarchically into a network of boulevards. An organism of this nature is clearly based on a profound trust that architecture – and the architect – can control the city, operating on a sort of blank slate to create a new cityscape. Meanwhile, the Indian culture has intervened profoundly on that of the Modern project, appropriating the area gradually over the last half century and creating a novel, idiosyncratic space. This may not be the "solution" the architect expected – or maybe it is; regardless, it is surely a "condition" that invites reflection. Alongside this process that involved so many works of the prolific Modern Movement, diverse expressions and philosophies developed

in the last decades of the 1900s that helped define a new vision of architecture, both as a professional practice and as the generator of an esthetic dimension.

Brutalism, for instance, at the end of the 1950s and Deconstructivism at the end of the 1980s both dared to propose a new esthetic. So distant from the canons of "the beautiful", which had remained integral to the poetics of the Modern Movement, this new style embraced imperfection, decadence and the fragility of contemporary materials.

In this context, the Japanese Metabolism movement of the 1960s should be seen as a separate phenomenon. Its manifesto specifically called on architects to design "megastructures" that can evolve "metabolically" (hence the name), adapting to the lifestyle of their inhabitants and thereby producing new forms of the city. Today, the greatest expression of this movement, Kurokawa's Nakagin Capsule Tower, stands half abandoned in Tokyo, a sort of ideological sanctuary for (us) fetishist architects. This secular sanctuary, with its extraordinary, poetic, heart-rending architecture, has deteriorated into a wreck simply because the planned-for upgrade and development project was never carried out, one which would have made the Tower a symbol of an extraordinary, poetic, heart-rending city in constant evolution.

Today we look at these urban relics with different eyes, not least thanks to the work of contemporary artists who have sought to change how we perceive expressions of imperfection, decadence and ruin. One particularly telling example of this is Dismaland, a revolutionary installation in West-on-super-Mare in England created by Bansky, an artist better known for his graffiti. Here Bansky proposes the experience of ruins as the central theme of an entire amusement park. It is communicated not simply by "admiring" artwork inspired by the theme, but more actively by relating to the decadent, imperfect, shabby employees and the intentional inefficiency of the organization. And yet, the depressing experience of this "bemusement" park has been sought out by thousands of people from all around the world.

Bansky's work is one more confirmation that a radical change in esthetic references has taken place in designing the constructed world, a transformation that allows us to feel more familiar with these types of presences. Thus we approach such symbols of failure with a greater sense of security, without feeling the need to conceal or destroy them. On the contrary, we accept them not only as elements of the landscape but also as part of our own environment.

These two terms may seem synonymous, and indeed they are often used that way, but their meanings are actually quite distinct. The term "landscape" refers to the *appearance* of a territory, so we could say it has a formal, esthetic and descriptive connotation. The meaning of "environment", on the other hand, is more complex, given that it is used in a wide variety of disciplines (from biology to mathematics) and is more a *set of conditions*, referring to the function and interaction of components; in short, it has a more structural connotation.

No doubt, all of us have experienced just how much contemporary ruins have become part of our landscape. To be able to act upon them through a mature plan, however, we must begin to consider them, with all their characteristics, as part of our environment, and become familiar with their fears.

AN INTERPRETATION
(OURS, THAT IS)

There are truly countless ruins left on the ground by our évolution over the last hundred years – countless and varied. Our research group Laboratorio di Innovazione e Ricerca sugli Interni (Lab.I.R..Int.) of the Design Department, Milan Polytechnic, has tried to catalog them, proceeding primarily with a taxonomy, which, however, turned out to be tenuous and ineffective. Subsequently, given the fragility, complexity and delicacy of so many of the issues involved, we opted for a more humanistic, literary approach, organizing them according to the underlying philosophy that – in our opinion – led to their failure. We began with projects that had failed because they were based on overly-optimistic predictions about the participants. We called this section "They thought they would be so many", and included projects ranging in size from small neighborhoods to entire cities, but all of which were simply too ambitious (of course this is easy to say with hindsight). These projects generated huge deserted settings, surreal landscapes of ghostly daily life.

Obviously, in this collection of stories of failures there are some whose lack of success was due to economic problems. The section "They thought they would become so rich" includes projects conceived to exploit a particular business that never actually materialized or, for whatever reason, collapsed miserably. Classic cases in this section include not only abandoned mines and bankrupt real estate investments, but even mad, poetic, self-declared micronations worthy of Don Quixote.

One of the characteristics of contemporary ruins is surely their powerful esthetic impact: surreal, poetic, heart-rending. It is often a question of ugly projects, in the broad sense, which are such an eyesore that we can hardly imagine how they could have been executed

with such a lack of aware-
ness. In the section "They
thought no one would re-
alize", we included huge
ideological monuments
(quite possibly used only
once), major production
plants that never produced
anything, and other situations bordering on, when
not exceeding, the limits
of legality – which explains
why some of these constructions have been torn apart,
torn down or demolished.
Nothing is so heart-rend-
ing as the failure of a project conceived for pleasure,
and yet this happens, too.
There are large-scale, even
enormous constructions
designed as places of en-
tertainment, which, for
various reasons, are now
deserted. The section "They
thought they would have so
much fun!" recounts cases
whose ruins arouse power-
ful emotions. In this section
of the book, images play a
particularly significant role,
powerful images such as the big wheels covered in ivy
and weeds or a fragile platform on the water that fright-
ened someone so much they knocked it down.
After an exploration like this, especially considering our
field of study in general and our approach to the disci-
pline in particular, how could we not finish with our own
proposal? In fact, the section "Now we'll take care of it!"
is devoted to a plan for a new urban scenario inspired by
a striking case of this type of abandonment. The aim of
the project is to respond to the problematic question of
architecture that has been abandoned, regardless of its
quality, with a proposal for a new urban typology.

A DIFFERENT WORLD TOUR

The ever-growing presence of these contemporary ruins around the world suggests to us that they must have an anthropological origin – that is, not a technical or economic one (at least not only). In brief, this abandonment should be considered as having an anthropological dimension. In fact, human beings have always abandoned their creations as they go along, moving onto the next one.

Today, however, we know how to build increasingly extraordinary buildings, but more importantly, we know how to and can document and share the abandonment. This analysis makes an enormous amount of information available in "real" time that used to remain buried in the memory of the local territory. In effect, there is a new "information" dimension that ensures that the ruins will not be forgotten or buried by providing a level of exposure through information and images, which allows the possibility of constant monitoring.

Such a dimension has never existed before in all of history. While it inspires interesting new reflections, this dimension does not foresee any "solution" (which may not be necessary anyway). On the other hand, as it makes information available for purposes of comparison, it ensures that future interventions can be adapted to the specificity of each case, enriching the field of options for the project in general.

It may be beneficial for planners to begin, as Franco Bolelli suggested, to "stop looking for solutions in the same drawer where the problems are". In fact, to find a solution to a situation generated by a particular system, it is surely best to look for it in a different system altogether, given that the first one did not work out.

They have fulfilled their destiny, so trying to resurrect these projects on the same foundations as always would be no more than a concession to nostalgia. In other words, we must make an effort to break away from the conditions that generated the problem in the first place and imagine new scenarios – and hopefully get them underway.

The increasing interest in these scenarios clearly reveals the emotional involvement they arouse. In fact, since our research team began to deal with this question, we have discovered that there are many enthusiasts around the world exchanging photographs of these scenes. And not only photos! Looking further, one finds a well-established network of information on how to reach these sites, whose appeal stems from their profound *pathos*, not from their "beauty". The magnetic attraction to these abandoned ruins is similar to what leads people to visit daunting cliffs that plummet down to cold shores, to cross torrid deserts, or to defy the tremendous pressure of the dark depths of the sea or the rarified atmosphere of bleak caves – in brief, those manifestations of nature that have always inspired passionate interest, altogether different from the gentler landscapes of mountain lakes, the hills of Siena or the beaches of the Caribbean.

Our contemporary ruins are to a metropolis like New York as a desert is to a beach with palm trees and azure waters. Just as there are groups of people who spend their free time (appropriately equipped) visiting inhospitable natural habitats, there are more and more groups of people (likewise well-prepared, also emotionally) who look for opportunities to be guided through man-made environments with abandoned or vacant buildings.

Given that there is always more "room for all" in this world, it is not absurd to imagine that a new international tourism will emerge – and in fact it already is emerging – with groups of company executives visiting derelict old factories or couples declaring eternal love in the streets of ghost towns or extended families celebrating birthdays in nuclear power plants that never started up. Come to think of it, it is not unlike the centuries-old tradition of visiting the Colosseum, which in the end is just an old abandoned stadium.

A DIFFERENT WORLD TOUR

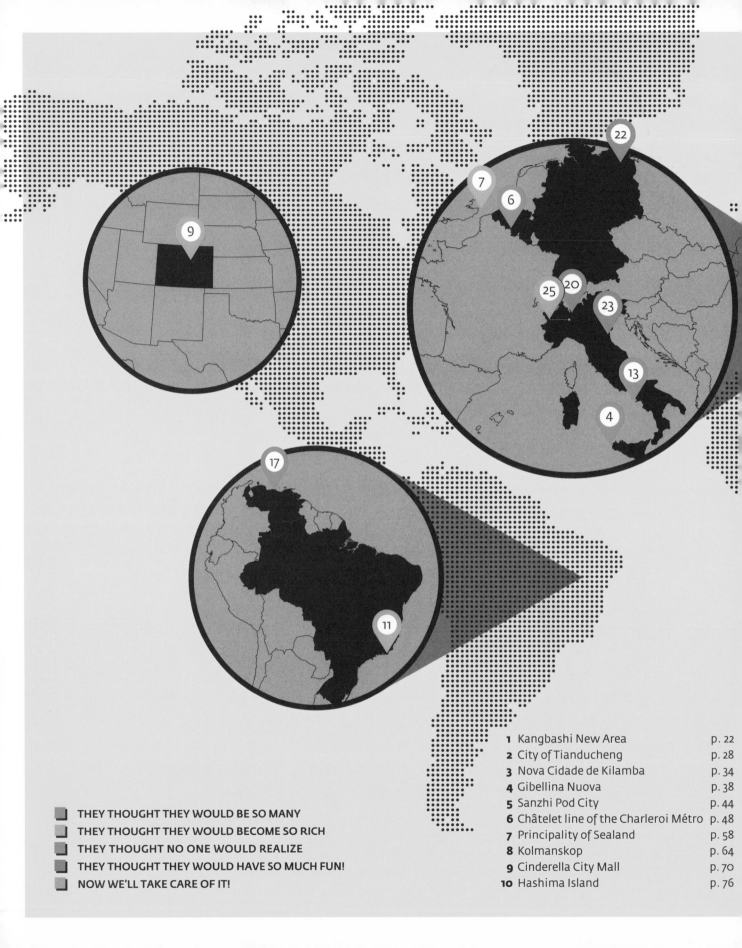

THEY THOUGHT THEY WOULD BE SO MANY
THEY THOUGHT THEY WOULD BECOME SO RICH
THEY THOUGHT NO ONE WOULD REALIZE
THEY THOUGHT THEY WOULD HAVE SO MUCH FUN!
NOW WE'LL TAKE CARE OF IT!

This section focuses on the most important element in any project that concerns a community: people. When there is a lack of people, the project has failed, but this is not like any other form of lack. Here, the actual motivation for human action is missing. So the failure is even more dramatic. Above all because a large, very large number of people are often envisaged, and when a project for so many people does not work because there are only a few of them, it is very depressing. In fact, the vistas of cities that have never become such are dramatic: designed for thousands, and at times millions, they remain uninhabited. Cities are the true expression of human evolution in the social sense, and only function if they are brought alive by people. A stunning beach is quite different, because our enjoyment of it is often threatened by the crowd, so in certain cases being alone enables us to enjoy the view, and the experience in general, more fully. In a city the opposite happens: an empty city is one that does not function. The experience becomes dramatic because the few inhabitants, when they do exist, wander through empty – and dangerous – neighborhoods looking for non-existent services. Indeed, no one would open a shop in a deserted city.

What is really striking is that these deserts are not, as often happens, caused by abandonment. People have never even wanted (or been able) to move there! This happens in all latitudes and in very different socioeconomic contexts, which makes them extremely depressing and disturbing. They have not functioned because they lack what should have been their raison d'être: to give individuals in a community a sense of belonging.

Such places are the three-dimensional representation of every architect's biggest nightmare in designing a new city, namely that it will remain uninhabited and be nothing more than an empty shell, a giant architectural model of the ultimate social project.

Behind a project there is always an idea, a utopia, a possibility. In this case the idea was that many human beings would agree with the choices made. *So they thought they would be so many.* But it did not happen, and these projects envisaged for large communities that were never built, wound up becoming desolate settings for a new kind of desert: the urban desert. (A. B.)

THEY THOUGHT
THEY WOULD BE SO MANY

KANGBASHI NEW AREA

Kangbashi New Area,
Ordos, China, Asia

Construction began
in 2004

Construction cost:
160 billion dollars
of public money

Kangbashi New Area, aka Hia Bagx New Area or Habagexi Subdistrict, is the most recent addition to Ordos – a city in Inner Mongolia, about 500 kilometers west of Beijing – and by far its least populated district. They started building Kangbashi in 2004. It covers a vast urban area, similar to that of a megalopolis, but to date is inhabited by only 30,000 people: a very small number compared to the number of buildings available, which in theory could house 1 million. The area surrounding the city is one of the richest in natural resources in China: around a sixth of the country's coal mines and about a third of its natural gas deposits are located there. The wealth deriving from the extraction of these resources has resulted in speculative building, supported by the Chinese government; in fact, 160 billion dollars of public money was allotted to the construction of this district. Kangbashi New Area was a major urban project devised by the Chinese government in the early 2000s, which aimed at constructing a new residential area, sell the housing and await the arrival of new inhabitants.

The squares are enormous, the roads unbelievably wide, the buildings unjustifiably tall. What is really weird is that the public services in the district function almost to perfection. An area with 30,000 inhabitants, which is more or less the size of a small mountain village in China, rarely has an airport, hospitals and various forms of public transport. These things function like clockwork in Kangbashi, but the fundamental element that would justify the expenditure of so much effort and state funding is missing: people. In effect the apartments of the many skyscrapers are mostly empty. The city can hardly be called such, since the typical orderly chaos of Oriental megalopolises is lacking: the cranes on the construction sites are at a standstill, waiting for new orders, and public spaces like the mosque are still closed.

At first the Chinese government planned to bring at least a million inhabitants to the new district in the southwest outskirts of Ordos, but this estimate was later reduced to around 300,000. However, sources of 2010 document 28,000 actual residents. A large number of the inhabitants of Kangbashi New Area are peasants from other parts of China, who have been forced to relocate to the aspiring metropolis following the government's expropriation of their land. This unfinished city, financed by earnings from coal mining, is beleaguered by all the problems of speculative building, compounded by the considerable volatility of the coal market, with its constant dips and peaks. Indeed, in Kangbashi you often come across posters with mug shots of builders and investors up to their ears in debt, who have fled the city.

If you're a videogame geek, Kangbashi will remind you of the mercantile House Ordos in the games based on the sci-fi *Dune* novels. But we're talking about the latest addition to the Chinese city of Ordos, located in Inner Mongolia. In one of the wealthiest areas of the People's Republic of China (it is estimated that a sixth of China's underground coal deposits are located here), there is a vast district that is actually uninhabited. Since 2010 economists, journalists and photographers have investigated this strange phenomenon, and in 2013 a British documentary *The Land of Many Palaces* was made. Recently, the prestigious daily *The New York Times* reported on the failure of this (potential) metropolis, and even went as far as describing it as a kind of "Disneyland, packed with kitsch monuments".

Ordos can be reached from the local Dongsheng airport. If you're coming from abroad you can fly to Taoyuan or Yinchuan airport, then take a short domestic flight, train or bus to Kangbashi.

Following pages: the Kangbashi Museum inspired by dunes and the National Library shaped like three books at an angle, are still waiting for visitors to arrive.

CITY OF TIANDUCHENG

Tianducheng, China, Asia

Construction began in 2007

Known as the "Chinese Paris"

Tianducheng is a city located in the suburbs of Hangzhou in Zhejiang Province, and covers an area of 31 square kilometers. Like many others in China, it is a faithful copy of a European city, a perfect reproduction of Paris in the Far East.

The city is characterized by the marked French style of the buildings, the various fountains in the squares and the manicured gardens in perennial bloom; it also has replicas of the Eiffel Tower and the gardens at Versailles.

The copy of the iconic tower in Paris is identical to the original, except for its height, which at 108 meters is about a third of its French equivalent. While strolling through the streets, you may also find yourself looking at a perfect replica of a fountain in the Jardins du Luxembourg, located in one of the main squares known as the Champs Elysées. They started constructing Tianducheng in 2007, with a population of 10,000 in mind. Despite the positive forecasts and economic boom that characterized China during that period, only a thousand people were living there in 2008. Today the residents number 2,000 and even the local media refer to this place as a ghost city. The lack of inhabitants is to be attributed to its location: surrounded by cultivated fields, it is difficult to reach except by winding country roads. With the passing of time the city has become a popular set for wedding photos and a surreal day-trip destination. While there, you may even see a coach with a liveried driver taking a bride and groom to the entrance of a yellow church at the top of a small hill, where a priest of Chinese origin performs Western-style wedding ceremonies in front of an altar with a crucifix. The shops are still vacant, while shanties and overgrown fields have begun to appear next to the luxury buildings, due to the exorbitant prices of the housing.

THINGS TO KNOW

In China they have not only reproduced the most famous amusement park in the world, but have also sought to replicate a whole city – with disastrous results.

This has given us Tianducheng, in the suburbs of Hangzhou, which can be reached from the local airport 27 kilometers east of the city center. This is not the first European city made in China, where, in fact, you can admire Florentia Village, clearly inspired by the cradle of the Renaissance; Holland Town in Pudong, and Thames Town, a faithful reproduction of British streets and architecture, not far from Shanghai.

Another "must-see" in Hangzhou is West Lake, inscribed on the World Heritage list, which has four islands. One of them has a particularly evocative name, "Fairy Islet", and has another lake on it: a combination that has given rise to the Chinese saying "in the lake there is an island and on the island there is a lake".

Left: replica, on a reduced scale, of the Eiffel Tower, surrounded by vegetable gardens and residential neighborhoods.

NOVA CIDADE DE KILAMBA

Nova Cidade de Kilamba,
Angola, Africa

Inaugurated on 11 July 2011

The new town was built in less
than three years by the state-
owned China International Trust
and Investment Corporation

Nova Cidade de Kilamba can definitely be described as a ghost town. Twenty kilometers from Luanda, the capital of Angola, it was designed to provide 82,000 homes in a 5000-hectare area covering 54 square kilometers, and to house the administrative headquarters of the recently created Belas district. It consists of 750 eight-story buildings, plus about a dozen schools and a hundred shops, all designed to accommodate half a million people. Nova Cidade de Kilamba was built in less than three years by the state-owned China International Trust and Investment Corporation.

The project is the result of an oil agreement between the Angolan and Chinese government. As the leading African oil exporter, Angola gave China priority access to this important energy resource and, in exchange, China agreed to build homes for half a million Angolans to combat the dire housing emergency in the country. In 2008, in fact, the Angolan head of state had promised during his election campaign to provide a million homes in four years. Thus the construction of Nova Cidade de Kilamba seems perfectly in line with the pledges made by the government, which describes the agreement as a winning political move, the project itself, however, reveals a few mistaken judgements. Indeed, the majority of Angolans still live in almost nomadic settlements with no electricity, no drinking water, no schools and no health services.

Despite this, Nova Cidade de Kilamba is the star of government promotional videos that show happy families enjoying a new lifestyle in houses with all the latest mod cons, far from the chaos of the capital and the shantytowns on its fringes. But these people are only actors, the truth is that from the time the first lot of 2,800 apartments was put on sale, only 220 have been sold to date. You rarely see cars and people in town, just one street after another and rows of uninhabited colored buildings. The only people you're likely to meet are Chinese workers busy finishing the last apartments. The commercial spaces are unlet: only one hypermarket has opened, near one of the entrances to the city.

Finding food to buy is often a well-nigh impossible task.

THINGS TO KNOW 🔍

Angola is not exactly around the corner, but if you get organized you can reach this country, which is one of the wealthiest in Africa and one of its leading oil exporters, not to mention the many fabulous diamond mines. This is also why the Angola pavilion at Expo Milano 2015 was one of the largest, while other African states were part of clusters.

According to Mercer, the UK financial analysis company, the capital of Angola, Luanda, was the most expensive city in the world in 2015, more costly even than New York and London.

All these resources could not have left the Chinese magnates indifferent. In fact, they precipitated to Angola, and also to other parts of Africa, where, in exchange for oil concessions, they have built entire cities like Kilamba, which is still too expensive for dwellers in this area.

GIBELLINA NUOVA

Gibellina Nuova,
Province of Trapani, Italy, Europe

Construction began in 1971, primary
urbanization was completed in 1976

Conceived by the mayor Ludovico
Corrao

In January 1968, the city of Gibellina was destroyed by an earthquake that struck the Valle del Belice, and was rebuilt only eight years later, but in another place and with a completely different identity. Yet 48 years after the quake, the new town still does not have a precise image. Described as an "open-air museum", Gibellina Nuova is based on a plan in the shape of a butterfly, symbolically linked to the souls of the dead, the psyche and rebirth.

Moreover, it conserves a host of works created by different artists so that the old city's soul might live on: at every street corner there are sculptures, buildings and art installations commissioned by the then mayor Ludovico Corrao to elevate the spirit of the new town through various contemporary visual languages.

The town has lots of open spaces, but the area is too large and the houses too far apart. It does not have a center that draws people together and also too few inhabitants for such a vast space, even if it is dotted with masterpieces. Following its reconstruction, Gibellina became a flourishing tourist destination, but the town soon went into a decline, since it was impossible to blend past and present. Today it attracts fewer tourists, having become something of a niche destination, but it deserves some kind of cultural recognition that would give the local economy a good boost.

Although it would like to remain an agricultural center, Gibellina Nuova is something completely different: it is informed by purely esthetic principles that are at odds with the life of its inhabitants, who are thus unable to identify with their area. An area which, despite the fact that it sought to combine landscape, town and architecture, appears to be in a limbo, alienating. Nothing more than a deserted town inhabited by mammoth artworks.

Gibellina Nuova is located 11 kilometers from Gibellina Vecchia, which was destroyed by an earthquake and abandoned. The alienating effect is created by the contrast between the lack of inhabitants – also before the quake – and the large number of works by prestigious artists in the half-deserted streets. Just to mention a few: Mimmo Paladino's *Mountain of Salt*, Mimmo Rotella's *City of the Sun* (*Tribute to Tommaso Campanella*), Pietro Consagra's *Star Steel – Entrance to Belice* and yet others by Accardi, Cascella, Pomodoro, Melotti and Mendini. Burri, one of the artists most in demand at contemporary art auctions, is also there with his *Crack*, which rises up from the ruins of Gibellina, firmly fixing the historical memory of the city.

Previous pages: some of the works of art donated to the town: an open-air museum whose upkeep poses problems.

p. 39: The sculpture *City of the Sun (Tribute to Tommaso Campanella)* by Mimmo Rotella (1987), behind the *Civic Tower* by Alessandro Mendini (1988), and the *City of Thebes*, a sequence of works by Pietro Consagra (1988).

pp. 40–41: Franco Purini and Laura Thermes, *The System of Squares* (1982–1991).

Left: the Mother Church designed by Ludovico Quaroni, which through the dome combines the symbolic perfection of the sphere, emblem of the universe and infinity, with the square, symbol of human perfection.

SANZHI POD CITY

Sanzhi, New Taipei City, Taiwan, Asia

Construction began in 1978
Demolished in 2008

Constructed as holiday homes for military officers posted to East Asia

The Sanzhi UFO Houses, also known as Sanzhi Pod City, are a series of abandoned pod buildings constructed in the Sanzhi District in New Taipei City, Taiwan. Sanzhi Pod City looks like something out of a 1960s–1970s sci-fi film, and is shrouded in mystery.

The buildings resemble the Futuro Houses designed by Matti Suuronen, some examples of which are to be found on the island of Taiwan.

The very unusual main entrance, which made the pods very popular with collectors, is reminiscent of an airplane door. The pod itself is made of fiberglass reinforced with polyester, polyester-polyurethane and polymethyl methacrylate, and is around 4 meters high and 7 meters in diameter.

Construction began on Sanzhi Pod City in 1978, and stopped in 1980. The idea of creating housing that was reminiscent of a UFO came from the Sanjhih Township plastics manufacturer Yu-chou Co., which was interested in finding new applications for its products. In the beginning, these homes were destined for wealthy inhabitants of the big cities who wanted to get away at the weekend.

They came into being as a holiday spot, adjacent to Tamsui, on the north coast, and became very popular with military officers returning from their postings in East Asia. The color of each building identified its position: those in the west were green;

those in the east, pink; the ones in the south, blue, and those in the north, white.

Architecturally speaking, the advantage of these modules was that others could be added to them, making each pod easy to enlarge.

This small luxurious holiday village also had a dike to protect it from the sea, marble floors in each house, an amusement park that was way ahead of its time, and other remarkable mod cons.

Nonetheless, the project was abandoned in 1980. According to local folklore, the site had been the burial place of Dutch soldiers, whose souls had in some way been disturbed by the construction work. It has also been suggested that the widening of a nearby road "bothered" a Chinese dragon sculpture, putting a jinx on the houses. Whatever the truth behind the legends may be, work actually seems to have stopped due to a series of financial problems. The Sanzhi UFO Houses remained uninhabited for over 30 years.

The buildings were scheduled to be demolished at the end of 2008, despite the fact that an on-line petition sought to save at least one of the pods and turn it into a museum. Demolition work began on 29 December 2008, and by 2010, all the UFO houses had been flattened and the site was about to be converted into a commercial seaside resort and waterpark.

None of this has yet been built.

For some it is an incredibly mysterious town that has sparked stories about aliens and paranormal phenomena, and for others, a classic example of an urban project gone wrong. In any event, what, on paper, was to have been a leisure spot for well-heeled weekenders in the area, ended up looking like an abandoned movie set.

If you take highway no. 2, heading east from Danshui to the north coast of Taiwan, you come to this place that seems to have been created by a set designer specializing in sci-fi movies, and which some see as inspired by retrofuturistic trends. It is located in the Sanzhi District of New Taipei, the most densely populated city in Taiwan – also known as Formosa or Republic of China (not to be confused with the People's Republic of China, which is somewhat larger and whose capital is Beijing) – which is rendered fascinating by its blend of ultramodern and historic past.

The UFO Houses, pod-shaped homes in Taipei's Sanzhi District, in a complete state of abandon prior to their demolition in 2008.

CHÂTELET LINE OF THE CHARLEROI MÉTRO

Châtelet Métro Line, Charleroi, Belgium, Europe

Construction began in the 1980s

Never opened to the public

The Charleroi Métro is famous because some of its branches were never built, partially constructed or finished, but never opened to the public.

The métro was designed in the 1960s, as a loop with eight lines radiating outwards and 69 stations to link the downtown area with the suburbs. Construction began in 1974, but only four lines are operating to date.

The abandoned Châtelet line of the Charleroi Métro, which is 6.8 kilometers long and has eight stations, was built at the beginning of the 1980s, but has never entered service.

Four of the stations on this ghost line have been finished, while the other four are at various stages of completion; its deserted rails and platforms have never seen a single passenger. All the stations were based on the same layout; the equipment had been installed; the signals and control systems worked, but before the line opened, people realized that the underground was of no use to anyone in this part of the city. Following the crisis in the steel industry in the 1980s and 1990s, the population had migrated, moved away for good. Thus the suburban lines disappeared, because the métro did not seem justified for a city with only 200,000 inhabitants.

Thirty years have passed, and nothing has changed: the line never entered service, nearly all the equipment has been stolen, the toilets and escalators appear to be working, but there is no electricity. The paintwork and tiles are still in good condition, although vegetation is gradually gaining the upper hand.

THINGS TO KNOW

Easy to get to, thanks to the second largest airport in Belgium located nearby, Charleroi is a city with just over 200,000 inhabitants. It is famous for one of the most terrible accidents in the 20th century: in one of its suburbs, Marcinelle, and more precisely the Bois du Cazier coal mine (which is now no longer in use and has become a UNESCO World Heritage Site), a fire broke out on the morning of 8 August 1956, causing the death of 262 workers.
Returning to the present, the métro line and stations in Charleroi are not the only ones to have been abandoned. Also in other parts of Europe, for example in two major cities like Paris and London, there are a few ghost underground stations: some have never been opened, others have been closed, yet others have been put to different uses.

This section is devoted to projects that bombed because they were money oriented. Projects that could have generated wealth, for the few or the many, but which did not develop in the right direction. Or did not develop at all.

But in their coming to nothing they did scratch, and sometimes gouge, the surface of the world.

The economy drives many projects, and always has done in the history of mankind. Many major expeditions were undertaken thanks to the financial support of people who hoped to find new markets from which they could profit. The fact that the explorers discovered new civilizations, which were so complex and different because human beings had organized themselves under other conditions, at times became merely a decorative, folkloric element. What interested these individuals, who in the future would be known as sponsors, was selling their products to new customers or securing new raw materials to their advantage – from Marco Polo's China to Christopher Columbus' America, just to mention two milestones in the history of the relationship between exploration and the market. The economy perhaps drives every project in which something is constructed, since constructing is an extremely important act that has always required a vast amount of resources, both financial and human. Major resources that are brought into play, often for a number of reasons: social, economic, cultural and so forth. When one of these prevails over the others, the whole project takes on a tremendous risk. The danger is that it will become more fragile, that it will fall apart when that one "pillar" collapses. In the cases in this section, that pillar is represented by economic issues. Thus we find small towns that were built near valuable natural resources and emptied out when these dried up, because there was no real sense of community, only major economic exploitation. Or projects that aspired to attract and create great new wealth, but in failing to do so simply remain crumbling ruins.

The following are places promoted by people, companies or communities who *thought they would become so rich*. But this did not happen, and we are left with these huge empty shells to look at and understand: minor deserts that are often surrounded by other deserts of sand or water. (A.B.)

THEY THOUGHT THEY WOULD BECOME SO RICH

PRINCIPALITY OF SEALAND

Sealand, North Sea, 10 km from
the Suffolk coast, UK, Europe

Built in 1942

A military platform outside British territorial
waters that became the "independent sovereign state" of Paddy Roy Bates and family

Sealand was originally HM Fort Roughs, built outside territorial waters in 1942 as one of the Maunsell sea forts that bolstered Britain's defences against German air raids. During World War II it housed around 200 members of the Royal Navy, but was abandoned immediately after the conflict.

The structure is composed of two huge pillars rising up out of the water, topped by a platform measuring over 1,300 square meters; it rests on a Royal Navy barge that was sunk, flooded and positioned on a sandbar now known as Rough Sands. There are no stairways and the platform can only be reached by being winched up on a swing seat. In 1966 it was occupied by Paddy Roy Bates and his family, a British citizen who was looking for a neutral territory from which to operate his pirate radio specializing in rock and pop. After consulting with his lawyers, he decided to occupy the platform, and then proclaimed it an "independent sovereign state" in 1967.

Thus Roy Bates became His Royal Highness Prince Roy and his wife, Princess Joan. This led to Sealand having its own constitution, flag, national anthem, postage stamps, currency, football team and five inhabitants. In 1968, Sealand engaged in its first international war: a British ship had approached to service a buoy near the platform and the inhabitants opened fire on the vessel. However, the British courts said they had no jurisdiction, because the incident had taken place outside territorial waters.

This independent state has not been recognized by any other nation to date.

The Bates family have come up with many ingenious projects over the years, which were often not realized or doomed to fail. From the casino in international waters to the attempts to create a safe house for businessmen and hackers, and to host servers and databases – a project that went under in 2008. Next they tried to sell souvenirs on their official website, and in 2013 there was a plan to store the "keys" to cloud, web proxy and VPN services and backup copies on hard disk.

The platform was also put up for sale, but it has still not found a buyer.

THINGS TO KNOW

Sealand is located six nautical miles from the Suffolk coast, east of the Thames estuary. It is a self-declared microstate, but not the only one in the world. There are in fact others in various parts of the globe, all created for the most diverse reasons: socioeconomic, propaganda or social protest, while others were inspired by literary works or movies, or founded for sheer amusement.

For example, the Grand Duchy of Westarctica in the frozen wastes of the Antarctic, which Travis McHenry declared an independent nation in 2001. It occupies a territory that could not be claimed by any country after the signing of the Antarctic Treaty.

Another example is Seborga, a little town with 300 inhabitants in the Province of Imperia in Italy, which has been demanding independence since the 1950s.

KOLMANSKOP

Kolmanskop, 10 km from Lüderitz in the Namib desert, Namibia, Africa

Constructed in 1908. Abandoned in 1954 when mining activity diminished

Built by the German government after the first diamond was discovered

Kolmanskop is a town located in the middle of the Namib desert, in southern Namibia, 10 kilometers from the port of Lüderitz.

It was built after Zacharias Lewala happened to find a diamond while working on the construction of the Lüderitz-Aus railway line in 1908.

Later it was discovered that the zone was rich in diamonds and it was proclaimed a Protected Area by Germany (of which it was a colony) and turned into a mine.

The mining activity brought rapid wealth, which was used to build a school, hospital, various shops, a theater, ballroom, gym, bowling alley, power station, ice factory, casino, as well as the first X-ray station in the southern hemisphere, the first tram line in Africa and a small railway station – all in the architectural style typical of German cities. The population was made up of 700 families of German miners, who extracted the diamonds directly from the sand, making a total of 1100 adults and 40 children.

Unfortunately the town was abandoned soon after it reached its zenith. The diamond reserves began to dry up after World War I and the town was abandoned for good in 1954.

Today Kolmanskop is a famous tourist destination. All that is left of its heyday are memories. The old houses of the pioneer miners still contain their abandoned furniture and utensils as a kind of testimony of times past, while the powerful desert is reclaiming what was once a part of it. The sand has penetrated the buildings, in some cases arriving halfway up the walls. It creates a surreal and spectral atmosphere that attracts photographers, film directors and travelers, so much so that ghost tours start from the center of Lüderitz every morning. They include not only a visit to the ghost town but also the museum that recounts the history of the diamond miners and of the town itself.

THINGS TO KNOW

Kolmanskop is Namibia's ghost town, located 10 kilometers from Lüderitz, one of the country's most important cities.

Lüderitz is also known as the "Munich of the desert" due to its typically Bavarian architecture. Indeed, the German influence is evident in different ways. Firstly, the name of the city (until 1883 it was called Angra Pequena: small inlet) derives from that of a merchant from Bremen, Adolf Lüderitz, who bought the land in the hope of finding precious metals.

Secondly, the main thoroughfare is called Bismarckstrasse, in honour of the prime minister who declared the area a German protectorate. There was no lack of clashes with the local population, which escalated into the genocide of the Herero and the Nama; in fact, on Shark Island, not far from the town, there is a concentration camp where the local rebels who fought with the colonizers were imprisoned.

The abandoned town of Kolmanskop, built in the German style with its sand-filled houses that make it a popular tourist destination.

CINDERELLA CITY MALL

Englewood,
Colorado, USA

Opened on 7 March 1968
Abandoned in 1995

The attractions included a handcrafted
Italian merry-go-round lit by 2,000 bulbs,
with room for up to 70 people

Cinderella City Mall was once the biggest indoor shopping center ever built between Chicago and Los Angeles. Arranged on three levels, the mall was inaugurated on 7 March 1968, after they had worked nonstop for three years to complete it. It all started in 1963, when a well-known developer, Gerri Von Frellick, made an offer to purchase the KLZ Tower on East Hampden in Englewood, Colorado. Opposition from residents in the area obliged Von Frellick to chose another location for the planned mall, this time on West Hampden. On 25 January 1965, the land was purchased for 1 million dollars, while it took another three years to finish the project.

When the Cinderella City Mall opened, it covered an area of more than 125,000 square meters. It boasted around 250 shops, various services and restaurants on three levels, as well as a theater with over 600 seats. From an architectural standpoint, the shopping center consisted of five individually named malls linked by a central covered courtyard known as the Blue Mall. A spectacular fountain rose up in the heart of the shopping center, soon becoming its most well-known symbol. A handcrafted Italian merry-go-round was set up at the mall: a double-decker with 28 hand-painted panels, it could hold as many as 70 people and was lit by more than 2,000 bulbs.

The Cinderella City Mall enjoyed tremendous success until the 1980s, when a downturn in the economy coupled with growing competition led many of the shops to close, and it was completely deserted in 1995. The Cinderella City Mall remained abandoned for nearly a decade. Starting in 2000, the city of Englewood sought to reuse the buildings that had been occupied by the shopping center and to upgrade the abandoned area. The mall was replaced by CityCenter Englewood, which houses the town hall offices, various shops, accommodation, a library and other municipal services.

BLUE

To reach Englewood, a town with a population of just over 30,000, and the Cinderella City Mall, your best bet is Denver International Airport. Aficionados of contemporary ruins will not want to miss this mall that was a record-breaking success but was abandoned from 1995 on, and experts on freemasonry and lovers of esotericism will go into ecstasies when they see Denver International Airport to which many websites on the genre are devoted. Its connections with freemasonry seem clear from the many murals that make reference to its symbols. But there are also people who are prepared to swear that its vast size (DIA is the largest airport in the United States and third largest in the world) was designed to hide something: a secret underground base managed by the New World Order together with, of course, extraterrestrial presences!

HASHIMA ISLAND

Hashima Island,
Nagasaki, Japan, Asia

Inaugurated on 7 March 1968
Abandoned in 1995

In 1959 it had the highest
population density in the world

Hashima is a man-made, one-kilometer-square island among 505 uninhabited islands in the Nagasaki Prefecture in Japan. It was built in 1810 over a large coal mine (owned by Mitsubishi), which, from 1887 to 1974, provided energy for the city of Nagasaki, located one hour away by boat. The mine was such a thriving enterprise that hundreds of apartments were built on the island for the miners, as well as schools, hospitals, gyms, cinemas, restaurants and shops for them and their families. Many of the buildings were actually the first reinforced concrete structures in Japan.

In 1959, Hashima had the highest population density ever recorded in the world – 3,450 hab/km². The apartments were reduced to tiny suffocating cells and residents divided into "castes" of single miners, married miners with and without children, Mitsubishi executives, and teachers. In its heyday, the island produced huge quantities of coal, though clearly at the expense of the quality of life of the workers.

When coal gave way to oil, Hashima was abandoned and Mitsubishi closed the mine in 1974.

Workers were entirely dependent on supplies from the mainland; in fact, many of them died of hunger or the effects of the appalling sanitary conditions.

Even though it was the site of so much suffering and death, Hashima has become a symbol for the Japanese of the country's postwar development. Today, the island is a graveyard of buildings doomed to collapse, but it is precisely this ghostly appearance that attracts filmmakers and enthusiastic explorers of urban landscapes. The collapsed façades reveal the interiors of apartments with their 1970s-style televisions and half-rotten furniture, not to mention shoes, bottles of shampoo, newspapers, and posters still hanging on the crumbling walls. In the deserted schools, decrepit desks and chairs are lined up in front of the blackboard exactly as they were 30 years ago when the last lesson was taught.

In 2009, a section of the island was partially reopened to the public.

The residential district on Hashima Island,
abandoned in 1974.

Hashima Island is twice the size of the Vatican City – a particularly fitting comparison since it is located in the Prefecture of Nagasaki, which was the hub of Japanese Catholicism. The island is now a cult destination for lovers of ruins and of industrial archaeology, the interesting and relatively new branch of archaeology concerned with evidence of industrialization. Since 2009, various tour operators have been organizing guided tours of the island, weather permitting, and that same year the Swedish film director Thomas Nordanstad, accompanied by an elderly inhabitant, shot a documentary there.

Hashima is often cited in various media, including TV programs, movies and videogames, and James Bond fans will recall some memorable scenes from *Skyfall* that were inspired by this contemporary ruin.

A must visit for the alternative tourist (but not only) passing through Nagasaki, Hashima – aka Gunkanjima (island of the warship) and Midori nashi Shima (island without greenery), became a UNESCO World Heritage Site in recognition of its historical and industrial importance.

A typical view of the residential district, designed to optimize the space on the island by accommodating as many residents as possible.

Previous pages: a group of tourists visiting the abandoned island.

TORRE ABRAHAM LINCOLN

Rio de Janeiro, Brazil, South America

Construction began in 1969

Approximately 250 of the 454 apartments have been bought

The Torre Abraham Lincoln, which was never completed, is located in the Barra neighborhood in the south-west of Rio de Janeiro, right next to its twin tower, which instead is inhabited and functions to perfection: the Torre Charles de Gaulle.

Each of the cylindrical towers is 110 meters high and has 37 stories and 454 apartments. Nowadays the Torre Abraham Lincoln is simply referred to as Torre H. The two round towers were originally part of a much larger urban development project for Barra, designed by Lucio Costa and Oscar Niemeyer at the end of 1960. Both architects were also responsible for the acclaimed planning and development of Brasília, with Costa designing the general layout and Niemeyer the individual buildings, as they did in Barra. Together they devised an ambitious plan comprising 76 circular towers grouped in "islands" of five or six, with wide expanses of greenery in between. Each island had its own shops, schools and the necessary services, also guaranteeing a view of the sea between one island and another and lots of fresh air. The full name of the requalification projects was the Plano Piloto da Barra da Tijuca. In those years, Barra was a fairly empty neighborhood and an ideal place for a building project, but the land, unlike that in Brasília, was privately owned, which meant that the impressive plans developed by Lucio Costa were optimistic, and probably unrealizable from the outset. Construction on the two towers began in 1969.

Many people bought apartments on paper, eager to move into their new property as soon as possible. The advertising posters were also full of enthusiasm and hype: "Paraíso Existe: está aqui!"; "Viva No Paraíso"; "A Nova Forma de Viver". But the project encountered various obstacles right from the beginning: the construction materials used were substandard, and people soon began to have doubts about the unconventional shape of the apartment blocks.

In 1972 building stopped due to structural problems. Moreover, the developer Athayde had used a legal loophole to transfer ownership to the buyers, which meant that the latter had to pay property tax even though they were unable to take possession of their apartments. Following this, Costa's impressive urban plan was ditched.

In 1980, Athayde announced that the tower would be finished, since they had managed to sell more of the apartments. Notwithstanding this, many doubted that the developer intended to complete the building. In 2004, the tower was occupied by more than 400 squatters, which resulted in Athayde declaring bankruptcy, thus avoiding any legal responsibility towards the owners of the unfinished apartments.

Approximately 250 of the 454 Torre H apartments are owned to date. The buyers are still waiting for them to be finished, but there seems no hope of this at the moment.

THINGS TO KNOW

Just as in the best families, where there may be one child who is virtuous and studies hard and another who is prodigal and spoilt, these twin towers could not be more different. Although we are talking about towers and not kids, the parallel remains: one, the Torre Charles de Gaulle, is complete and functions perfectly, while the other, the Torre Abraham Lincoln (aka Torre H), has never been finished. The edifices are in the Barra neighborhood in Rio de Janeiro. The beauty of this city, which was the capital of Brazil before Brasília, can be evoked by naming just two things: the statue of Christ the Redeemer, one of the seven wonders of the modern world, and Copacabana, the beach where thoughts inevitably turn to sex. As everyone knows, there are far more attractions, which, together with the many flights available to Brazil, is a real invitation to go there.

The twin towers side by side: the Charles de Gaulle that works and the Abraham Lincoln that is unfinished.

NEFT DAŞLARI

Neft Daşları settlement,
Caspian Sea, Azerbaijan, Asia

Construction began in 1949

It was the largest undersea oil
deposit in the world

The first town to be built in the middle of the ocean, Neft Daşları (Oil Rocks) is located in the Caspian Sea, 42 kilometers from the coast, at the eastern-most tip of Azerbaijan. Construction began in 1949, near vast undersea oil fields that had just been discovered. Seven ships in disuse, including the world's first oil tanker constructed by the Nobel brothers, were sunk to provide the foundations on which the first of the structures supporting the platforms were constructed.

Later all kinds of facilities were built on the platforms: two autonomous power plants, boilers, oil-gas processing stations, drinking water facilities, hostels and apartment blocks up to nine stories high, cultural and recreational centers, hospitals, a bathhouse, training school for oil riggers, bakery, canteen, lemonade factory and a landing strip for helicopters. There were also two undersea oil pipelines and even a park with trees, and a mosque.

The 1960s were the settlement's "heyday": then it could accommodate 5,000 people and was the largest undersea oil field in the world, both in terms of the amount of oil and volume of raw material produced. Today, however, access is limited.

In the course of 60 years, over 170 million tons of oil and more than 15 billion cubic meters of natural gas were produced.

The settlement is now composed of over 200 fixed platforms. The metal roads that link the various zones cover a total length of more than 350 kilometers, but most of them are collapsing, posing a great danger to shipping. There are no permanent residents and around 2,000 people work shifts on the rig, staying for a fortnight each month.

Geologists estimate that a reserve of 30 million tons of oil remains. When it is exhausted, the structure could become another ghost town, especially considering that the infrastructures are old and will last a decade at the most.

Neft Daşları, an hour from Baku by helicopter, was the first settlement built in the sea. Connected by metal viaducts, it can accommodate 5,000 inhabitants.

The screenwriters of the James Bond series must be particularly fascinated by towns built in the sea. In fact, while the artificial island of Hashima inspired some of the scenes in *Skyfall*, the Neft Daşları complex, which lies about 40 kilometers from the Apsheron peninsula on which Baku, Azerbaijan's major oil producer is located, provided the setting for some of the scenes in *007 The World Is Not Enough*.

From the first half of the 19th century, geologists had noted various expanses of rock with an oil patina in this area in the middle of the Caspian Sea, which revealed the presence of many deposits beneath the seabed.

Once the eagerly awaited permits were obtained, exploratory drilling began, incentivized by the postwar five-year Soviet plans designed to increase the production of crude.

Recognizing the importance of these reserves, Nikita Khrushchev promoted the construction of more comfortable accommodation, as well as facilities like a hospital, bakery and even a city park. All in exchange for tons of oil.

It is unlikely that this place could exist in its own right, without being dependent on the extraction of oil. In all probability it will become another ghost town but, with reserves of black gold still amounting to around 30 million tons, this is not going to happen any day soon.

The platforms of which the town is composed are linked by hundreds of kilometers of metal roads, half of which are now unusable due to corrosion and a lack of maintenance.

This section is a bit different, since it is devoted to "eyesores", in the broad sense. In fact, we are not proposing a strictly esthetic interpretation although, however debatable, it would not be devoid of meaning. We are offering a broader esthetic reading that encompasses the ugly, the hideous and the unacceptable. Put like that it could seem facile and capricious, but if we extend the context to the more cultured and sensitive terrain of art, the examples are many, even without counting the most experimental and aggressive expressions of contemporary art. Suffice it to mention the compelling canvases by Sironi – now displayed in the leading intellectual salons – which represent desolate, polluted working-class neighborhoods from which the inhabitants dreamt of escaping (and they did on a Saturday afternoon, thanks to the trams that took them downtown). The damage has already been done. So we need have no qualms about citing these cases that touch on, and sometimes exceed, not only the limits of esthetics but often those of legality.

Huge edifices built to represent an ideology, some of which were never finished, others never used (or maybe just once …). Grotesque, anomalous landmarks, huge blots on surreal landscapes. Ideology is often imposed and supported by a strong and, at times, authoritarian central power. But this phenomenon can also start from the "bottom", fuelled by an anomaly in the system. Something that creates the conditions for people to organize themselves independently, generating a kind of "coral reef", inhabited by communities that are "different" from the host system. The rules will also be different. The communities will also grow in a different way. The "coral reef" that contains them will also be different. Many of these projects are described as ecomonsters. A word coined for – so we could say in "dishonor" of – the Hotel Fuenti in Vietri sul Mare on the Amalfi coast. It was built illegally at the end of the 1960s, which made it the subject of a long environmental dispute that ended with its partial demolition at the close of the 1990s.

Sometimes ugliness takes shape and is developed, and always because *they thought no one would realize* … But then somebody does realize, the issue has to be faced and there are two possibilities: demolish it (the easier option) or take it as an opportunity (a far more difficult challenge). (A. B.)

THEY THOUGHT
NO ONE WOULD REALIZE

HOTEL DI ALIMURI

Vico Equense, Province of
Naples, Italy, Europe

Building permit issued in 1964
Demolished because it was
dangerous on 30 November 2014

Thanks to 60 kilos of explosive,
the ecomonster was reduced
to dust in 12 seconds

This ecomonster, built overlooking the sea near Alimuri beach, was the focus of environmentalist and legal battles for years.

The hotel's story began in 1964, when the Vico Equense City Council issued a permit to build a 5-story hotel complex on the edge of the coast. The 16-meter high building was to have a volume of 18,000 cubic meters, an area of 2,000 square meters, 150 rooms and an Olympic-size swimming pool. Some time later, work was stopped when the steep cliff of the promontory rising up behind the site became unstable. Three years later another building permit was issued so that work might be resumed, but after various interruptions, it was stopped once and for all in 1986, because the cliff had to be strengthened. The situation was aggravated by the slow collapse of the floor and the gradual disintegration of the rock face behind. Meanwhile, the building not only became increasingly precarious and dangerous, but was also used as a garbage tip. All that remained was the skeleton of what was to have been a luxury hotel. Despite the fact that access was forbidden, it became a nocturnal haunt for ravers and a summer attraction for daredevil divers, who launched themselves from the crumbling floors, resulting in many accidents, some of which were serious.

In 2003, the first in a series of meetings was held at the Regional Council of Campania to initiate the extensive requalification of the area, which included the strengthening of the promontory, the relocation of the structure and the demolition of the part already built. However, the destruction of the skeleton was only decided on jointly by the Ministry for the Environment and the relevant provincial and regional bodies in 2007.

At the end of November 2014 – 50 years after the story began – 1,200 explosive charges weighing 50 grams each and amounting to 60 kilograms in all, were inserted in the foundations, and the ecomonster was reduced to dust in just 12 seconds before an enthusiastic crowd.

THINGS TO KNOW

The term "ecomonster" is used to describe a building that is incompatible with its surroundings, in other words a structure that is a blot on the landscape. We do not know exactly who coined the neologism, but it appears to have been used for the first time by a well-known environmental association to describe a hotel on the Amalfi coast.

Italy is often referred to as "Bel Paese", which means beautiful country, but despite this appellative created by Dante and Petrarch, who knew a thing or two about beauty, the country is full of these eyesores.

Italy with its many statelets and thousands of belltowers is united when it comes to discussing archiflops. From Milan to Palermo, there are any number of completely abandoned buildings and others that were never finished, which have endured for decades, also because of the endless red tape involved in obtaining their demolition.

Only in a few cases, like Alimuri, is the ecomonster tamed and vanquished.

The skeleton of the hotel on the Alimuri coast that blotted the surrounding landscape for 50 years.

Following pages: the demolition of the ecomonster on 30 November 2014.

RYUGYONG HOTEL

Pyongyang, North Korea, Asia

Construction began in 1987

This edifice was declared a failure by the North Korean authorities, which led the government to deny its existence and distribute modified maps and manipulated images that "documented" the absence of more than 300 meters of reinforced concrete.

In the mind of the North Korean government, the Ryugyong Hotel, on which construction began in the mid-1980s, was to be the tallest hotel in the world and the seventh highest building on the planet. The hotel is a 105-story skyscraper 330 meters tall with a floor area of 360,000 square meters, which makes it the largest edifice in the Democratic People's Republic of Korea. The building consists of three wings, each of which is 100 meters long, 10 meters wide and inclined at an angle of 75 degrees. It was to have housed restaurants, casinos, discos, offices and 3,000 rooms, with an estimated construction cost of 750 million dollars. However, it did not become a symbol to be proud of, because it is still waiting to be opened to the public.

It was built by the dictator Kim Jong-il – father of the present North Korean leader Kim Jong-un – as an answer to the opening of the Westin Stamford Hotel in Singapore, erected in 1986 by the South Korean SsangYong Group and recognized as the biggest hotel in the world that same year. During a period in which the influence of the Cold War was still strongly felt, the only way the government saw to beat the South Korean capitalists was to show its technological superiority by drawing up a building program that would be completed in a maximum of two years. But something went wrong: in 1992, the project was still not finished but the money was, and this giant structure remained without windows and interiors, electrical and plumbing systems for 16 years. All because of a severe economic crisis in the country, following the collapse of the Soviet Union, which also resulted in construction companies using shoddy materials.

Work resumed in 2008, thanks to an Egyptian telecommunications company named Orascom, which invested a huge amount of capital (around 140 million dollars) in the North Korean building sector, thus permitting the top floors to be remodeled. The upper floors and one side of the hotel were faced with glass panels, which enabled Orascom to obtain various concessions for the installation of phone aerials on the top of the Ryuoyong Hotel. All this gave good reason to hope that the building would be completed in 2012, the centenary of the birth of the "Eternal Leader" Kim Il-sung, but there has been no inauguration to date, instead the building is still incomplete.

Pyongyang holds many records: it is a cultural and commercial center, a leading industrial city and the most densely populated city in North Korea, of which it is the capital.

Although tourism is on the increase, few Western travelers go to what is one of the most impenetrable countries in the world. The iron-clad dictatorship, which controls every aspect of human life, does not offer visitors much freedom. Indeed, they come up against endless barriers: they cannot enter South Korean territory, journalists need a special visa and further restrictions are imposed on American and Israeli citizens. This enigmatic country has another intriguing aspect: although it is led (with extensive powers) by Kim Jong-un, the de jure president is Kim Il-sung, who died in 1994 but is immortalized as eternal president in the constitution.

The Pyongyang cityscape with the giant 105-story hotel shaped like a pyramid, which was never finished.

Following pages: after the building had been abandoned for 16 years, the Egyptian company Orascom changed the look of the hotel by installing glass panels all around the upper part and on one of the sides.

COMMUNIST PARTY HEADQUARTERS

Buzludzha, Bulgaria, Europe

Construction began in 1974

The story goes that a time capsule illustrating the meaning of the building is buried in the cement used to construct it.

Formally known as the House-Monument of the Bulgarian Communist Party, the building looks like something out of a 1950s sci-fi movie. Situated on Mount Buzludzha at a height of 1,441 meters and 12 kilometers from the Shipka Pass, it is the biggest building ever constructed in Bulgaria for ideological and propagandistic purposes. Perched on a high promontory in the Balkan Mountains, the monument looks like an enormous flying saucer made of cement, complete with a slogan praising the Communist Party.

In 1891, after the last Turks had been expelled from Bulgaria following 500 years of Ottoman rule, it was here on Mount Buzludzha that socialist revolutionaries like Dimitar Blagoev met in secret to lay the foundations of the Bulgarian Social-Democratic Workers' Party, precursor to the Bulgarian Communist Party. The House-Monument of the Bulgarian Communist Party opened 90 years later, in 1981, to celebrate both the country's liberation from Ottoman rule and the 1944 victory over Hitler's Nazi domination of Bulgaria. The building soon became the Bulgarian Communist Party headquarters, and there is a colossal statue of Blagoev in the monumental entryway.

The construction of the building was made possible by government funding and by donations for a total of around 14,186,000 levs (about 7 million euros). The monument was designed by the architect Georgi Stoilov and it took seven years and 6,000 workers to build it, led by General Delcho Delchev, head of the Stara Zagora civil engineering section. More than 60 Bulgarian artists were involved in the design and execution of the mosaics and paintings representing the themes central to traditional Soviet propaganda, such as the family, the revolution, the battle between rich and poor, the war against capitalism, and even space travel. There are also portraits of former Bulgarian Communist Party leaders inside. The Soviet star that adorned the building's tower was three times as big as the one at the Kremlin and, at its zenith, the monument was considered one of the major icons of the communist world. After the collapse of the government in 1989, this building owned by the Communist Party was inherited by the state in 1991. From that moment on it gradually fell into a decline. The portraits of Todor Zhivkov and his daughter Lyudmila were destroyed immediately. The copper decorations inside were stolen and the building is slowly crumbling; robbers and vandals constantly damage the windows and steal what is left of the mosaics.

Today, the monument is completely abandoned and no public institution seems to be concerned with its conservation or renovation. Even the large red star that surmounts it is peppered with bullet holes.

Overall view of the Bulgarian Communist Party
Headquarters, which was inaugurated in 1981 and is
now totally abandoned – as is evident from the state
of the congress hall (previous page) and the belvedere
(following pages).

At first glance it looks like an UFO that has landed on the top of Mount Buzludzha – former arena of the fighting between the Ottoman Empire and the last Bulgarian rebels – but it is actually a representation of the megalomania of totalitarian regimes, as well as an example of waste not to be imitated.

The monument was inaugurated in 1981, on a mountain that could only be reached by a side road from the Shipka Pass 12 kilometers away, which linked the province of Gabrovo to that of Stara Zagora. It has now been completely forgotten, even by the Bulgarians themselves, and is abandoned, leaving it prey to acts of vandalism. The latest insult came from some wise guy who defaced it with the slogan "Enjoy Communism" in the same lettering as that of the ultrafamous American beverage. But then again we are in Gabrovo, the capital of humor and satire.

CRIMEAN ATOMIC ENERGY STATION

Kazantip, Crimea, Asia

Construction began in 1982

It is in the *Guinness Book of Records* as the most costly nuclear reactor in the world

The unfinished Crimean atomic energy station is located on the Kerch peninsula, on the banks of the Aktashskoe saltwater lake, that was to be used for cooling purposes.

Work began in 1975 with the construction of its satellite town Shcholkine, designed to house 20,000 inhabitants and nuclear scientists. Work on the plant itself began in 1982. It was designed to supply the whole peninsula with electricity and to provide the basis for further development in the metallurgical, engineering and chemical sectors in Crimea.

A special crane was installed in the reactor building of the first unit, to shift materials and assist construction and assembly inside the reactor area. The first unit of the plant was 80% complete and the second unit 18%, when construction was interrupted for various reasons. The country's economic situation was very unstable, the Chernobyl tragedy was still fresh in people's minds, there were protests from environmentalists and the plant's site was risky from the geological and seismic standpoint.

This atomic energy station is in the *Guinnness Book of Records* as being the most costly in the world. After it was abandoned, projects were developed to use it as a training center for nuclear power station operatives. Later, with the slogan "Nuclear party in the reactor building", it became the venue for the Kazantip Festival that took place in the turbine hall from 1995 to 1999.

Today, hordes of tourists from all over the world visit the plant, taking advantage of the fact that it is the only one that you can enter, to have a truly unique experience and see what remains of the symbols of the Soviet Union.

Currently, from a distance the power station looks intact, but from close up you discover it is only a shell.

Shcholkine has not become a ghost town thanks to its strategic position near the sea, but its initial population has halved.

THINGS TO KNOW

There is an unfinished atomic energy station 170 kilometers from Sinferopol, the capital of the Republic of Crimea. Nearby stands the town of Shcholkine, named after the Russian physicist Kirill Shchelkin, which was to house the plant's workers.

Talking of atomic power stations, particularly in Ukraine, we automatically think of Chernobyl and the disaster of 26 April 1986, one of whose consequences was to boost the anti-nuclear movement that had begun in the 1970s. In Italy, in just a few months, over a million signatures were collected for the 1987 referendum that led to the abandonment of nuclear energy. The fear of another tragedy after Chernobyl was one of the reasons why the Crimean plant was never completed.

But the memory of what happened in 1986 doesn't seem to have had any effect on the local younger generation, in fact, from 1995 to 1999, the Kazantip Festival of electronic music was held in the plant, considered by those who surf the internet "the wildest party in the world".

This image of the Crimean atomic energy station at Kazantip could be misleading, since it gives the false impression that it is still in use, but the previous photos show that it has been totally abandoned. Even the crane was removed and sold in 2003.

TORRE DAVID

Caracas, Venezuela, South America

Construction began in 1990

The American TV series *Homeland* devoted an episode to the Torre David

The Centro Financiero Confinanzas, also known as the Torre David, is a 45-story skyscraper for offices in the city of Caracas, designed by the famous Venezuelan architect Enrique Gómez. However, it remained unfinished following the death of David Brillembourg, the man who originally conceived it, in 1993, and the Venezuelan economic collapse in 1994.

It is the third highest skyscraper in the country, after the twin towers of the Parque Central complex. Construction began in 1990, but work was halted in 1994. It was to have housed the head offices of Brillembourg's bank, until a banking crisis brought the country's economy to its knees.

The building is lacking lifts, electricity, running water, windows and some dividing walls are unfinished. The whole complex consists of six buildings: El Atrio (lobby and conference room); Torre A, 190 meters high, consisting of 45 storys and also including a heliport; Torre B; Edificio K; Edificio Z and a 12-floor car park.

The tower was first occupied by groups of squatters in 2007, and later by over 2,500 families.

What had begun as a temporary tent city has, over the years, turned into a flourishing, highly organized community, under the strict management of an ex-convict, Alexander "el Niño" Daza. The inhabitants of the surrounding neighborhoods have reported that the tower has become a kind of safe house for gangsters and other criminals. Since it was abandoned, the families living illegally in the Torre David have transformed the unfinished building into a vertical slum, complete with food shops, tattooists, internet cafés and a hairdresser's. The residents, in a sense, completed part of the work that was interrupted, as they managed to bring running water up to the 22nd floor. They could use motorbikes to get up and down the first 10 floors, but they had to use the stairs for the upper levels. Some residents even had cars parked in the building's garage.

Over the years the tower has taken on various contrasting guises. It has been described as a paradise for drug lords and for the murderers in the TV series *Homeland*, praised as an experiment in social responsibilization at the Venice Architecture Biennale and featured in countless articles, publications and documentaries. On 22 July 2014, the Venezuelan government launched "Operation Zamora 2014" to evacuate hundreds of families from the tower and relocate them in new buildings in Cúa, south of Caracas, as part of the Great Housing Mission project. By April 2015, around three quarters of the families had left the tower and the last inhabitants were relocated in July of the same year.

Before definitive eviction in 2015, it was considered the largest occupied building and tallest slum in the world. In 2012 it was awarded the Golden Lion at the Venice Architecture Biennale for the best project representing the theme of Common Ground as an example of informal group living. Certainly informality was not lacking in a skyscraper that housed many shops and activities of various kinds, even including some dentist's surgeries, which were all illegal. Easily reached by many direct flights, Caracas is a city whose exoticism and extraordinary beauty will win you over.

The illegal residents of the Torre David in the corridors of the Caracas skyscraper during the peaceful eviction on 24 July 2014.

Previous pages: the façade of the tower, originally built for offices, turned into a vertical slum by the residents, who completed and personalized their homes.

KOWLOON WALLED CITY

Hong Kong, China, Asia

Demolished in 1993

Called "The city of darkness": the buildings were so close together that the sunlight couldn't filter through

For decades, Kowloon Walled City was the most densely populated spot on the Earth, a teeming labyrinth with more than 300 interconnected skyscrapers. Constructed without the benefit of architects or engineers, these buildings housed apartments, commercial spaces and every type of activity imaginable, including crime. Although the walled city was "home" to 33,000 people, most Hong Kong residents dared not even come near it. This city within a city came into being after the 1898 agreement, which ceded Hong Kong to Great Britain for 99 years, excluding, however, Kowloon Walled City. Founded during the Song dynasty, Kowloon served as an outpost for the military defending the area against pirates and supervising local salt production. Later, when the Japanese occupied Hong Kong during World War II, a number of Kowloon's buildings were demolished to provide construction materials for the nearby airport. After the occupation ended, the city's population grew exponentially, with thousands of squatters moving into the abandoned buildings.

In the end, Kowloon Walled City became a haven for criminals and drug addicts who lived here beyond the reach of the law.

Thus, beginning in 1980, Kowloon was famous for its brothels, casinos and opium dens. Wandering through its alleyways, it was not unusual to stumble upon makeshift butcher shops selling dog meat. Kowloon Walled City figured at the heart of a diplomatic crisis between Great Britain and China, each of whom refused to take responsibility for the tragic conditions in the city, where, among countless other problems, only on the roofs could you find some fresh air and escape from the claustrophobic, often windowless apartments. Eventually, the British and Chinese governments agreed to demolish the Walled City entirely. Many residents protested against this drastic decision, and in fact the government was forced to pay out 2.7 billion Hong Kong dollars in compensation. Evictions began in 1991 and were completed in 1993.

Seen from a rooftop in Kowloon, the only place where it was possible to breathe and escape from the dense congestion (see previous pages).

THINGS TO KNOW

Kowloon was an actual city within a city, at least until 1993, when it was razed to the ground. This part of Hong Kong had earned itself the nickname "The city of darkness", which was very appropriate, since for years it had been a place without any order or control by Britain, which from 1898 ruled Hong Kong for 99 years, or by the People's Republic of China, to which it was transferred to on 1 July 1997.

At the end of the 1980s, over 33,000 people were living in 2,185 flats. In addition to the crumbling buildings and widespread crime, there was the problem of overpopulation, which made Kowloon one of the most densely populated places in the world. However, this jumble of houses, people and objects, widespread crime and total lack of social policies did not prevent some of the inhabitants from having fond memories of the place. Like Albert Ng Kam-po, today the pastor of the evangelical community, who, in an interview for the *South China Morning Post*, speaks of his childhood spent in Kowloon as being a happy time.

There was also a feeling of solidarity in this environment beset by crime and poverty. The people, as Ida Shum, an elderly woman from Kowloon, remembers, were always there for you and helped each other despite the terrible conditions they lived in.

Here more than ever the images speak for themselves. This section contains projects devised more or less for amusement. Projects that would see happy children on rollercoasters and smiling adults, who might steal a kiss at a certain point. In any event, people who came to these places to have fun, who were seeking to escape from the daily grind of work, problems, homework... Unlike this image of people enjoying themselves, in some cases the party is over, it's like walking down the street through confetti and the debris of merrymaking, the morning after carnival celebrations. In others the party never even began, like in those films where the bride or groom doesn't show up at the altar. Everything is ready for the wedding, from the grandmothers in their hats, to the bridesmaids and the savouries for the reception... Then there are the cases where the party was interrupted, even if it was in full swing. Everyone was having a whale of a time, but then the neighbors called the police who put a stop to it all.

Every culture and society provides entertainment, whatever form this may take. Whether it be the private celebration of a wedding anniversary or festivities involving millions of people. We have all had this kind of experience, so it is even sadder when we recognize the signs of enjoyment that no longer exists or perhaps never began. These are those desolate experiences that a genius like Banksy has stored in his imagination so that he could create his greatest – at least to date – temporary installation *Dismaland* at Weston-super-Mare in the UK. You won't find it here because it wasn't a flop, quite the contrary, it was a resounding success! Thousands of people set off between 21 August and 27 September 2015 on an uncomfortable journey, to visit a sad park that offered an agonizing experience of crumbling Disney castles, princesses in road accidents and deliberately rude entertainers.

These settings evoke a Fellinesque atmosphere, situations where *they thought they would have so much fun*, perhaps they did, but then it came to an end. It's a bit like the mood you experience walking along the beach of a bathing establishment out of season. (A.B.)

THEY THOUGHT THEY WOULD HAVE SO MUCH FUN

NARA DREAMLAND

Nara, Japan, Asia

Opened in 1961
Closed on 31 August 2006

It was to be a Japanese Disneyland, but its creator did not manage to get permission to use Disney characters

Nara Dreamland is an abandoned amusement park in the city of Nara on the Japanese Island of Honshu. On 31 August 2006 it was closed for good, but not demolished.

It was built in 1961 and directly inspired by a famous amusement park at Anaheim in California. In fact, it contains copies of various attractions in the American park including Sleeping Beauty's castle, Adventureland, Skyway, Submarine Voyage, the monorail, a pirate ship and so on.
Even the entrance is a faithful replica. The main attraction was the switchback called Aska, made entirely of wood. It was 1,081 meters long and a little over 30 meters high. The trains had seven carriages each of which could accommodate four people and were able to reach a speed of 80 km/h. Nara Dreamland has an unusual history. In the second half of the 1950s, Kunizu Matsuo, a Japanese businessman, visited the United States and was very impressed by the Disneyland in California. He decided that Japan too should have an amusement park that was just as spectacular. He contacted Walt Disney directly in order to devise and construct the first Japanese Disneyland at Nara, the ancient capital of Japan.
But this dream never came true. When construction work was nearing completion, they couldn't agree on the licence's price for using Disney characters in Nara Dreamland. So figures were created by famous Japanese designers, including Anpanman, a famous manga character invented by Takashi Yanase, but the style of the buildings and the attractions closely resembled those in Disneyworld. The park opened in 1961, but it began to go into a decline 22 years later, when the Tokyo Disneyland opened. The number of visitors dropped to such a degree that the park was bought by a Japanese supermarket chain in 1993 and closed 13 years later.

THINGS TO KNOW

An amusement park where there's not much fun to be had. None at all, in fact.

Empty streets, abandoned merry-go-rounds, rusty games, not a place where a kid would spend a happy time. This desolate scene is to be found at Nara, the ancient capital of Japan on the Island of Honshu, declared a UNESCO World Heritage Site in 1998.

You can reach the city by taking the Haruka Limited Express from Kansai International Airport to Tennoji station and then the train to Nara on the JR Yamatoji line.

Though Nara Dreamland is no longer a suitable place for kids, it has become a popular destination with travelers attracted by its ghostly atmosphere. They like to savor it in the early hours of the morning or at dusk, when they can wander freely through the rubble of what was once Sleeping Beauty's castle or the hotel that once welcomed tourists. Undisturbed, the curious who love contemporary ruins are sure not to bump into anyone, not even Ran-chan and Dori-chan, the two park mascots that used to welcome visitors.

The Aska switchback, made entirely of wood, is over a kilometer long and 30 meters high. It was the park's main attraction. Today the structure is overgrown with thick vegetation.

CONSONNO

Consonno, Province of Lecco, Italy, Europe

The "Città dei Balocchi" was built in 1962

Consonno was abandoned due to landslides in 1976

Consonno is a little medieval village mentioned for the first time in a scroll in 1085. Located in a green valley not far from Milan, it had 200 inhabitants at the beginning of the 1960s. They were all farmers, but none of them owned the house they lived in or the fields they worked in.

On 8 June 1962, Count Mario Bagno bought the whole village intending to create an amusement town in the Brianza hills. In order to execute the project, bulldozers demolished the whole place leaving only a church, a small cemetery and the priest's house. Instead of farmhouses and stalls, a 30-meter-high minaret, a Chinese pagoda, a luxury hotel, shops, gaming halls, an open-air dance floor, even a medieval castle, fountains, Egyptian sphinxes and a faux cannon all sprang up in the space of five years.

A hill was even flattened to improve the vista towards Monte Resegone.

The "Las Vegas of Brianza" also included a car racing track, football and basketball fields, a mini-golf course and a zoo.

The postcards of the time said "The sky is bluer at Consonno" and "It's one big holiday at Consonno", capturing the organizers enthusiasm for the festive atmosphere. But in 1976, when the novelty was beginning to wear off, the tourist flow dropped considerably; moreover, that same year a landslide destroyed the only access road, which was not rebuilt until 2007.

In 1981, Bagno made another attempt to relaunch the town by converting the Hotel Plaza into an old people's home, but the facility moved to Introbio in 2006.

The following year the town was completely trashed during an illegal rave party.

In 2014, because the owners had put the village up for sale, the last four inhabitants were given eviction notices.

The dream lasted less than a decade and the now abandoned "Città dei Balocchi" has become a ghost town. Today the vegetation continues to invade the dilapidated buildings and the only people you find are visitors curious to see and photograph what remains of the town.

Like the Spreepark in East Berlin and Gulliver's Kingdom near Mount Fuji in Japan, this is an amusement town that entertained many families for a few years and that is now abandoned with some buildings being used as cowsheds. The idea was a dream child of the 1960s economic boom, when Count Bagno bought a whole village that was then destroyed to make way for an amusement town.

After years of abandon and some destructive incidents, the future of Consonno is in the hands of Olginate Town Council.

After its sale had been announced and then denied on the internet, a well-known figure, Francesco Facchinetti, known as DJ Francesco, stepped in and suggested forming a group of entrepreneurs who would buy Consonno and make it a university center with various courses on offer.

The Consonno minaret is really and truly the landmark of what was to be the "Las Vegas of Brianza".

GULLIVER'S KINGDOM

Kamikuishiki, Japan, Asia

Opened in 1997
Closed in 2001

The amusement park is near the forest
of Aokigahara, known for its large
number of suicides

Gulliver's Kingdom is a theme park located two and a half hours from Tokyo, which has a 45-meter statue of Lemuel Gulliver stretched out on the ground. The park was short lived since it only lasted four years, from 1997 to 2001, when the lack of visitors forced the owners to close it down.

The construction of Gulliver's Kingdom was financed by the Chuo Bank Niigata, that became bankrupt because of a series of unpaid debts. The park was therefore put up for auction by the Kofu district court, but no one offered the minimum price of 3.1 billion yen. A second auction, where the price was lowered to one billion yen, closed on 8 November without any offers, thus sealing the park's fate.

Though located at the foot of the magnificent Mount Fuji, Gulliver's Kingdom was forced to close because of its unfortunate position. For some twisted and mysterious reason, the owners decided to construct the park in the Aokigahara region, where the centuries-old forest of the same name is sadly notorious for its high suicide rate every year. In addition to this, the nearby village of Kamikuishiki is home to the Aum Shinrikyo sect and also has a plant for the production of nerve gas. Its adepts used the Sarin gas produced there to kill 19 people, 12 of them on the Tokyo Metro. On 22 March 1995, the sect headquarters was attacked by over a thousand police officers wearing full gas masks. When the park was opened in July 1997, the village inhabitants hoped it would help to erase the negative image of the place.

The park offered visitors some unusual amusements. The attractions most similar to those that we normally expect to find in an amusement park were bob-sleigh and sledge runs – not exactly ideal for small children. But the main attraction was certainly the enormous statue of Gulliver positioned right in the middle of the park, the site of countless tourist photos. From its closure until 2007, the year it was demolished, the park remained abandoned, a favorite destination for lone explorers and vandals in search of spaces to take over.

Gulliver's Kingdom, now abandoned, stands at the foot of Mount Fuji, which is considered a holy mountain by Shintoists, who believe it their duty to make a pilgrimage there at least once in a lifetime.

Aokigahara, also known as Jukai (sea of trees) clashes with the beauty of the volcano as it did with the park's function when it was open. This lush forest is sadly notorious for being the favorite place for those intending to commit suicide; the practice is actually so widespread that the authorities have put up notices (also in English) to dissuade them. Various ways may be used, but the suicide rate here is the second highest in the world after the Golden Gate Bridge in San Francisco.

A view of the village with Mount Fuji in the background.

Previous pages: Gulliver lying among the houses in the now abandoned park.

SPREEPARK

Berlin, Germany, Europe

Built in 1969
Abandoned because of a lack
of visitors in 2001

It was the only amusement park in the
German Democratic Republic

Spreepark, the first and only amusement park in East Germany, was constructed in Berlin by the communist government in 1969. Also known as Kulturpark Plänterwald, after the name of the district where it was located, it was a must visit for all the families in the German Democratic Republic for years.

The amusement park, characterized by a big wheel 45 meters high, visible from afar, had merry-go-rounds, rollercoasters, streams and kiosks, and is located in 295,000 square meters of greenery. The plan was very simple and the independent attractions did not give the idea of a single fantastical world, but after the park became unified, various natural elements were introduced – such as lakes and green areas – as was a single entry ticket. Later, however, because the ticket was so expensive, Spreepark began to attract fewer visitors and, after the fall of the Berlin Wall, the park was less popular.

At the beginning of the 1990s, the whole area became an environmentally protected site. The hectares of the amusement park were further reduced, making it impossible to create the necessary infrastructures for it to function.

In 2001, Spreepark closed and turned into a ghost park, becoming a favorite destination for urban explorers from Berlin. A place full of huge dinosaurs, dead merry-go-rounds, abandoned swan-shaped boats and a dilapidated big wheel, all overgrown.

Just before it closed down for good, the Berlin government had renovated the whole structure to get it in working order again, but because of debts it was put up for auction via an advert on the Internet. One night in 2014, Spreepark was almost entirely destroyed by a raging fire. Since then, it has ceased to be an attraction even for the groups who visited it secretly or the guided tours organized at weekends.

There was not much fun to be had in East Germany under one of the most repressive dictatorships of the 20th century, and particularly in Berlin, a sad, divided city. But it was here that the first and only amusement park in the German Democratic Republic was constructed in 1969.

Now that it has been abandoned, it can be recommended to those who love Dario Argento films and Dylan Dog atmospheres, and not even the fire that broke out in 2014 or the guards have discouraged intrepid urban explorers. They climb over and crawl under fencing, anything to get a thrill out of this place, which was used as a set of the film *Hanna*, starring Cate Blanchett, in 2011. In addition to the cinema, crime too has shown an interest in Spreepark. Some years ago the park's managers sent some attractions in containers to Peru, claiming that it would be cheaper to have them repaired in South America, but five years later, in 2006, they were condemned for drug trafficking. It seems the containers were also used for transporting drugs.

Some of the attractions of the amusement park in an obvious state of abandonment in 2014, before the fire.

REPUBBLICA DELLE ROSE

11.6 km from the coast of the province of Rimini, 500 m from Italian territorial waters

Built in 1966
Demolished with explosives in 1969

In 1968 the engineer Giorgio Rosa announced the birth of the Repubblica Esperantista dell'Isola delle Rose

The Isola delle Rose is the name of a 400-square-meter man-made platform in the Adriatic Sea, nearly 12 kilometers from the Rimini coast, outside Italian territorial waters.

The project was realized by a Bolognese engineer, Giorgio Rosa, after various on-the-spot inspections in the area.

The actual construction took several years due to adverse weather conditions, which meant work had to be interrupted. Nonetheless, by 1965, a light and very resistant platform was ready and in 1966 it was definitively anchored to the seabed. The 20x20-meter platform, made of reinforced concrete and steel, supported by nine pylons planted at a depth of 40 meters and 8 meters above the surface of the sea. It had a kind of bar-cum-restaurant, a post office, and an area with quays and steps for boats dock. Originally the construction was to have five floors.

On 20 August 1967, the island was opened to the public. Easily accessible from the Italian coast, it drew hordes of visitors who arrived by boat.

In 1968, Rosa proclaimed himself president and announced the birth of an independent sovereign state called the Repubblica Esperantista dell'Isola delle Rose on the platform. The new state had a government, a currency, a flag, a national anthem and a small radio station. It minted its own money and Esperanto was the official language. It also issued postage stamps and had 62 square kilometers of sea, but it has never been formally recognized as an independent nation by any country in the world. The Italian state viewed the project as a ploy to avoid paying taxes on the money made from tourists. Consequently, in June 1968, Isola delle Rose was occupied by the police and subjected to a shipping block. In the winter of 1969, the navy blew up the platform with two controlled explosions of 526 kilos of TNT each.

The sinking and subsequent dismantling took around forty days, but there are still some remains of the platform in the sea.

The engineer Giorgio Rosa may have repented of his project which, after some decades, he described in an interview as "a sin of ingenuousness", but it has certainly intrigued filmmakers and writers, even years later.

This imaginative idea (it was 1968 and the imagination was king) to create a microstate with Esperanto as the official language, became the subject of a documentary by Stefano Bisulli and Roberto Naccari in 2009 and a book by Walter Veltroni published in 2012.

The national anthem, taken directly from *The Flying Dutchman* by Richard Wagner, would also have pleased those more refined ears who have always criticized the Italian national anthem by Mameli.

The mini-republic was located a little over 11 kilometers from Torre Pedrera on the Rimini coast.

On this and on the previous pages: some details of the Italian police monitoring after the declaration of the independent Repubblica delle Rose, as documented by *Panorama* of 11 July 1968.

WONDERLAND

Chenzhuang Village, China, Asia

Demolished in 2013

Was designed to be the biggest amusement park in Asia

Wonderland, designed as an amusement park but never completed, was located about 32 kilometers from the Chinese capital Beijing. Its designers intended it to be the stunning Chinese answer to Disneyland: a magnificent theme park capable of attracting millions of visitors every year, in a fairytale setting, in some respects a bit kitsch to our eyes.

Originally with the financial backing of the Reignwood Group, whose head office is in Thailand, it was designed to be the biggest amusement park in Asia, covering an area of 120 acres. Construction work stopped in 1998, due to a dispute between the developers and the landowners, which brought to light a corruption scandal involving even key figures in the Communist Party, so much so that the sudden abandonment of this massive building project raised concern about a real estate bubble in China. In 2008, an attempt was made to relaunch the construction work, but it failed.

The abandoned buildings included a fantastic entrance that was to welcome visitors, beyond which was a ghostly world of unfinished medieval edifices, reminiscent of an enchanted village. The worst thing was the castle, the symbol of Wonderland, which was a half-built skeleton standing alone in its unfinished glory. Some daring people have climbed the castle's turrets and from that height they could admire the whole park in all its desolation. After being abandoned for 15 years, it became a favorite place for graffiti writers. Squatters also occasionally lived in some of the buildings, and the farmers who owned the land took over some areas for planting crops.

Over the years, the theme park became very famous among filmmakers because of its ghostly atmosphere; this feeling was enhanced by the disturbing masks for children that lay around on the floors of the buildings. It could have been the setting for an episode of *Scooby Doo*!

Another strange thing is that some people have reported seeing parking attendants in the car park, presumably waiting for visitors. The unfinished abandoned structures were demolished in May 2013, thus eliminating any hope of the park reopening in the future.

THINGS TO KNOW

Sinister creaking, skeletal old buildings and a permanent fog shrouding everything: this couldn't be further from the festive image of an amusement park. Yet it has happened to what was designed to be the biggest theme park in the whole of Asia, covering an area of 48 hectares and less than an hour from Beijing. But the kids for whom the park was planned don't seem to mind the sinister atmosphere of the place and many of them, mostly the children of local farmers, go there all the same and invent games to pass the time, while their parents are working in the fields. The organizers of Wonderland wanted it to be the Chinese answer to Disneyland, but it wasn't.

NOW WE'LL TAKE CARE OF IT!

TURNING
PROBLEMS INTO
OPPORTUNITIES

No, what you are about to read is not positive thinking. Because being positive is obviously all very well, but if you don't have a strong vision and don't work damn hard, then positive thinking is as useful as a bicycle without wheels. It's rather a question of vital thinking. It's a question of seeing clearly that – as in the natural order of things – the biggest opportunities often arise from problems, failures, ruins. That's true of our choices in every field, it's true of relationships, it's true of sports (Michael Jordan wasn't joking when he said "I've missed more than 9,000 shots in my career ... And that is why I succeed"). It's true of societies and cultures and thought systems. What catastrophists – and the sad theorists of the downtrend – don't understand is that so often the end of something is simply the beginning of something else, that one thing stops existing or growing, and other unexpected things take shape and lead us where we would never have imagined. Because when we are capable of maintaining and if

need be developing a strong vital drive, then aches and pains and falls may hurt really badly, but we can use them to grow.

It is – as Alessandro Biamonti explains so brilliantly – a physiological process for architecture. Where flops and wrong predictions and expectations, abstruseness or simple obsolescence are as frequent as leaves falling in the autumn, and where the opportunity to reinvent and reconstruct is considered timely, if not natural. In this respect, the project for the Torre Galfa by this group of students from the Politecnico is by no means an abstract exercise. Because it emerges from very real needs, desires and possibilities, and because they have developed it with great inventiveness. I know that what they have imagined will never happen, but if one had the courage to carry out an operation like this, what a big success it would be!

TORRE GALFA

The Torre Galfa, built between 1956 and 1959, is one of the most important ruins of Milanese contemporary architecture. Impressive and ghostly, it made a comeback in the media when part of the Macao group of artists occupied it in May 2012. Located at the intersection of Via Galvani and Via Fara, in the heart of the then burgeoning Milan business district just a few steps from the Pirelli skyscraper, it was designed by Melchiorre Bega and consists of a low main block and a 103-meter-high tower. It is built of reinforced concrete with an aluminum framed glass façade and its pure lines are reminiscent of the International Style. Described by Giuseppe Vaccaro as "the most chaste of the Milanese skyscrapers", it was admired by Gio Ponti for the perfect proportions of its volumes and recognized by Bega himself as being the skyscraper "that has the simplest lines". It was built as part of that Milanese cityscape in which the skyscrapers represented modernity, also because of their strong technological impact. It was not merely by chance that Michelangelo Antonioni shot some scenes of the 1961 film *La Notte* on the seventh floor of the tower, which he turned into a hospital. The tower is characterized by its severe, pared down interior, which has a sequence of floors, organized on a grid of 75-centimeter squares. The offices of different sizes are open plan, arranged flexibly according to a modular system. The tower was originally built to house the petrol company Sarom and when it was later taken over by the Banca Popolare di Milano in 1980, some structural changes were made to the basement and low main block.

The rest of the building kept its open plan design divided by mobile partitions, which was not altered over the years by the maintenance work and upgrading of the various systems that the tower underwent. The bank occupied the building for 25 years, until it was handed over to the real estate company Immobiliare Lombardia, controlled by the insurance group Fondiaria-Sai. It was then that it began to go into decline, despite the fact that the new owners had started procedures for its renovation. In actuality, the work that had been announced was never undertaken and the tower fell into disuse.

Though it is typical of the image of postwar Milan and it is an example of technological and building development during the last century, the tower is not considered of historic and architectural interest and therefore not protected by regulations regarding development. During the latest work on the building, the interior partitions were removed, the floors and the underlying layers were taken up, thus exposing the reinforced concrete slab, while the curtain wall remained intact. The façade has deteriorated considerably, in fact the ceramic tesserae covering the structural elements are either stained or missing and the metal frames show surface wear and tear. The present state of the building and the absence of legal protection mean that the façade risks having to be completely replaced. The intention not to make changes in the architectural structure, expressed in the requalification project recently drawn up by the Gruppo Unipol and the Milan City Council, will be proportionate to the degree of sensitivity shown in the interventions on the exterior.

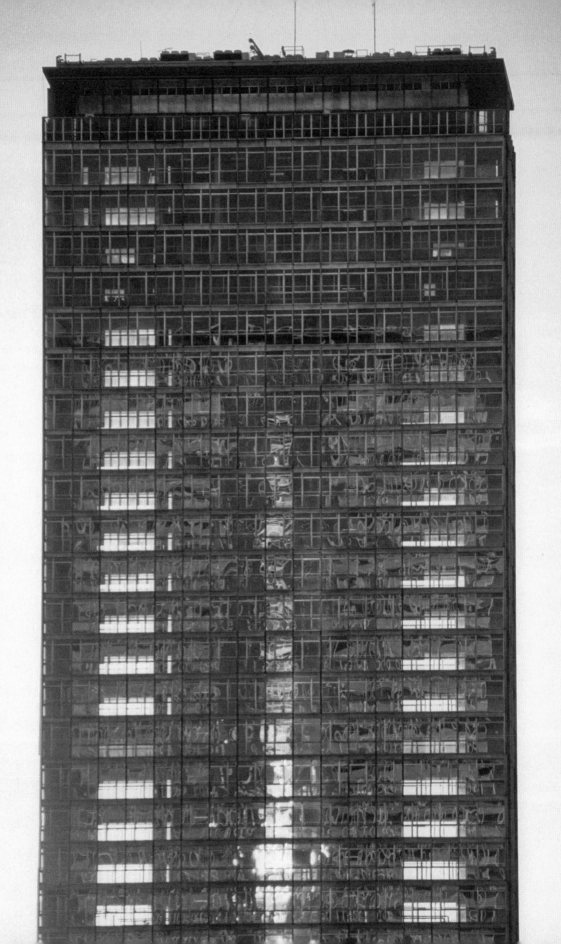

THINGS TO KNOW

The example for this initiative was the occupation of the Teatro Valle in Rome, whose purpose, according to those who organized the action, was to denounce the lack of shared spaces and was applauded by the Nobel Prize winner, playwright and actor Dario Fo. The occupation of the Torre Galfa was aimed at creating a place where artists could experiment with new languages and develop alternative projects.

It all came to an end on 15 May 2012, when the tower was peacefully vacated. But there still remains the problem of what is to happen to the many empty buildings, which becomes even more complicated since no institution has ever actually counted them.

A VERTICAL URBAN PARK

When faced with this beautiful abandoned tower, your mind begins to visualize possibilities. Just like in Leopardi's poem *L'Infinito.* In the poem he imagines a sea behind the hill where it would be sweet to be shipwrecked, in this case we are faced with a transparent parallelepiped that emerges like a large void in a densely solid urban context. Hence, looking at this empty interior, "In my thoughts I imagine" that something unexpected may happen. Something that, emerging from the logic of the design, could explore a new way of interpreting these buildings, by considering them elements of a new anthropized nature, which may be given new functions. So here is the proposal for a vertical urban park. We asked our young designers to think of the functions often present in large urban parks, to develop them and organize them following the vertical sequence of the tower.

We asked them to give the city a new reference model.

I think the students had fun and ended up exhausted after the workshop, where they produced some wonderful projects that have been exhibited several times, greatly sparking the public's interest.

They thought about everything that happens in an urban park and the new tower that they imagined had the following: places for artistic performances, new spaces for and ways of providing even do-it-yourself refreshment, sport as a great indoor activity, music in all its forms from the radio to the silent disco, ateliers for creative workshops, a complete urban farm, areas for bookcrossing and emerging forms of publishing, an onsen with a Zen garden, an interesting free zone around a botanical garden growing illegal plants, an

exciting adventure ride winding round the tower like a snake … It would have been nice if someone had got engaged during the workshop, but I don't think it happened (I live in hope).

PROJECTS BY

B. Camporelli, V. Canapini,
A. Cantelli, G. Canziani,
A. Capasso, G. Capitani,
G. Carignani, D. Castiglione,
C. Cattani, D. Ceriani, A. Chan
Maomei, F. Cocco, F. Coccolo,
V. Colangelo, C. Concilio,
S. Consonni, L. Corgniali,
L. Cotini, M. Cremona,
M. Crespi, F. Cristofolo,
M. Dassi, R. De Iuliis,
M. Dente, S. Derosa, F. Dileo,
S. Di Maria, D. D'Ingeo,
D. Di Stefano, F. Donna,
S. Elli, L. Failoni, E. Fallani,
M. Fanti, G. Fasiello

A HALF-SERIOUS GLOSSARY

Amusement park

A recreation area that differs from a funfair in that it is not a random collection of individual entertainments, but typically an enclosed park equipped with a variety of often thematic amusements that the visitor is able to enjoy, usually by paying an entrance fee. This kind of park, the first of which was Disneyland that opened in the United States in the 1950s, has developed considerably, occupying vast areas of land that are difficult to reconvert if the park closes down.

▲ *Nara Dreamland; Consonno; Gulliver's Kingdom; Spreepark; Wonderland*

Communist Party

The political party whose thought was founded on Marxist-Leninist analysis and on the pursuit of a communist society which led – in Europe – to the founding of the Soviet Union, aka the Union of Socialist Soviet Republics. Disbanded in 1991, after the fall of the communist regime, the party left countless testimonies of its prolific building activity, both residential and public, which clearly reveal inadequacies and signs of abandonment.

▲ *Communist Party Headquarters; Crimean Atomic Energy Station*

Demolition

An action designed to remove edifices or structures that are deemed inappropriate, mainly by using explosives or bulldozers. The more euphemistic term is "dismantling", while "blasting" is used when explosives are involved.

▲ *Hotel di Alimuri; Sanzhi Pod City; Kowloon Walled City; Repubblica delle Rose*

Deterioration

This can happen to parts of structural elements and also to whole buildings and districts, seriously compromising their original functions. The consequences of this are often a serious threat to the surroundings.

▲ *Châtelet Line of the Charleroi Métro; Cinderella City Mall; Communist Party Headquarters; Gulliver's Kingdom; Spreepark; Nara Dreamland; Wonderland*

Ecomonster

A neologism coined for the Hotel Fuenti on the Amalfi coast. It indicates an edifice or group of buildings that are considered blots on the landscape. In the majority of cases the hope is that they will be blasted (see also: Unauthorized construction, Demolition, Skeleton, Unfinished construction).

▲ *Hotel di Alimuri*

Economic boom

First used to define an Italian and Japanese period between the 1950s and 1960s, the term generally refers to a time of strong economic growth, often accompanied by major technological innovations and big investments in public and private real estate. These investments create market conditions as dynamic as they are fragile, which can cause a real estate bubble.

▲ *Kangbashi New Area; City of Tianducheng; Nova Cidade de Kilamba; Sanzhi Pod City; Torre Abraham Lincoln*

Economic crisis

Often linked to a recession (which is what happens in the United States when GDP diminishes for two trimesters in a row), the term is used to define a period characterized by major negative economic factors that have serious repercussions at the business and social level. These are one of the main reasons that certain building operations remain incomplete, or entire districts and towns are abandoned.

▲ *Gulliver's Kingdom; Nara Dreamland; Crimean Atomic Energy Station; Sanzhi Pod City; Cinderella City Mall; Torre Abraham Lincoln; Neft Daşları*

Futuristic

Something that could be realized, given the right circumstances, but which remains within the realm of the possible and will not necessarily be completed. The term is often associated with the sci-fi literary genre, and also with some buildings whose concept is inspired by an improbable vision of the future that is often so far removed from reality that it is bound to be inadequate.

▲ *Sanzhi Pod City; Gibellina Nuova; Communist Party Headquarters; Consonno; Repubblica delle Rose*

Ghost tour

The name for a profitable tourist business that has become a big thing in recent decades, and consists in a visit to an abandoned site that is thought to be haunted. Visitors are usually accompanied by a guide who recounts stories and legends about the ghosts that inhabit the place in question

▲ *Nara Dreamland; Consonno; Kolmanskop*

Ghost town

An abandoned town. The causes are many, and ghost towns are to be found all over the world. Some have become major tourist attractions, frequently due to the presence of interesting buildings or elements that mark a precise moment in history.

▲ *Kolmanskop; Hashima Island; Consonno*

Landmark

A point of reference that is interesting from a historical or esthetic standpoint, or a feature of the landscape. In an urban context, the term has recently been associated with imposing new constructions. Some unfinished or abandoned buildings have, in fact, become important urban landmarks.

▲ *Hotel di Alimuri; Ryugyong Hotel; Communist Party Headquarters; Principality of Sealand*

Landscape protection

The *landscape* represents the esthetic and cultural aspect of the environment, which consists in its anthropological, physical, biological and ethnic components. Its protection is enshrined in the constitution and regulated by laws, and entails the difficult task of preserving its characteristics and reconciling them with human action.

▲ *Hotel di Alimuri; Hashima Island; Communist Party Headquarters; Consonno*

Microstate

The term came into usage in the second half of the 20th century, and indicates those often self-declared nations that cover a particularly small area, sometimes no more than a few hundred square meters. These mini states often have their own currency, postage stamps, passports and titles – noble and honorific – just like any other nation.

▲ *Principality of Sealand; Repubblica delle Rose*

Real estate bubble

A particular kind of speculative bubble, which is generally produced by an economic boom and is characterized by a rapid hike in real estate prices. Such a period is often marked by a specific kind of real estate activity involving new constructions that are particularly prone to abandonment, especially after the bubble bursts and prices drop, with evident socioeconomic consequences. Real estate bubbles have often left buildings, and sometimes whole districts, abandoned.

▲ *Kangbashi New Area; City of Tianducheng; Nova Cidade de Kilamba; Sanzhi Pod City; Torre Abraham Lincoln*

Requalification

In architecture, town planning and related disciplines, an activity aimed at improving the quality of a building, neighborhood or area through the use of design tools that are not limited merely to technical interventions on structures and materials, but also embrace changes in use and socially innovative projects.

▲ *Torre David; Torre Galfa*

Ruin

The remains of man-made constructions that are in a state of abandonment. The causes can be many and linked both to major natural phenomena and to changes in the community that has produced them.

Skeleton

Also known as a *structural frame*, it is the load-bearing structure that supports the building and various weights (people, furniture and fittings, machines etc.). Often consisting of a structure of beams and pillars resting on the foundations, the skeleton is what is left in view if the building is unfinished (since it is constructed first) and in many abandoned edifices (since it is the most solid part).

▲ *Hotel di Alimuri; Torre David*

Squatter

From the verb to squat, it is someone who occupies, without the rightful owner's permission, parts of an abandoned building or land with a view to requalifying them and living there, or for productive and cultural purposes. Many countries have sought to regulate these illegal occupations.

▲ *Torre David; Kowloon Walled City*

Territorial waters

The part of the sea, near the coast, over which a country can exert its territorial sovereignty in the same way that it does over land. Since 1982, every country has been free to establish the extent of these waters, within 12 miles of the low tide line.

▲ *Principality of Sealand; Repubblica delle Rose*

Unauthorized construction

A criminal offence that consists in constructing a building without the necessary permits. As well as blighting the landscape, such operations have seriously endangered hydrogeological stability, in some cases putting the resident population at risk.

Hotel di Alimuri; Kowloon Walled City

Unfinished construction

A building, bridge or other structure on which work has not been completed. When this is for financial reasons, construction is rarely resumed. There also exist buildings that were not finished for reasons linked to history or to the actual design. One of these is the Sagrada Família, on which work began in 1882 and continued almost nonstop (except for the Spanish Civil War).

▲ *Hotel di Alimuri; Torre Abraham Lincoln; Torre David; Crimean Atomic Energy Station; Ryugyong Hotel*

Urban exploration

Also known as Urbex or UE, it is the exploration of man-made structures in a state of abandon. Although it has been undertaken for around two centuries, Urbex is currently in the media spotlight, because there are more opportunities to document it photographically or on video.

▲ *Châtelet Line of the Charleroi Métro; Hashima Island; Kowloon Walled City*

Graphics, layout and illustrations
Alice Beniero
Translation
Susan Ann White, Felicity Lutz and Lauren Sunstein for Scriptum, Rome
Editing
Anne-Kathrin Gräfe

The original Italian edition was published in 2016 under the title "ARCHIFLOP. STORIE DI PROGETTI FINITI MALE. Guida semiseria ai più clamorosi casi di errore, fallimento e sfiga in architettura" by 24 ORE Cultura, Milan.

© 2017 Niggli, imprint of bnb media gmbh, Zurich
www.niggli.ch
ISBN 978-3-7212-0960-0

1st edition 2017

Picture Credits

© Remi Benali / Corbis: 88–89
© Giorgia Canino: 40–41
© ChinaFotoPress / ChinaFotoPress via Getty Images: 29, 32–33
© Michael Christopher Brown / Contrasto: 23
© Simone Donati / TerraProject / Contrasto: 39
© Leo Erken / Laif / Contrasto: 87
© Simon Fowler www.simon-fowler.co.uk: 59–63
© Athanasios Gioumpasis / Getty Images: 157–163
© Greg Girard, Vancouver: 129–134 and back cover (r. b.)
© Jörg Glaescher / Laif / Contrasto: 109
© Dawid Gusiak, Canterbury: 139–145 and back cover (r. a.)
© Stefano Gusmeroli MilanoFoto.it: 179–181
© Cristian Hernandez / Anadolu Agency / Getty Images: 124–125
© Jauder Ho / Getty Images: 46–47
© Hoberman Collection / UIG via Getty Images: 65–69
© Imaginechina / Contrasto: 26–27; 30–31
© Impact Press Group / NurPhoto / Corbis: 110–111
© Kevinhung / Shutterstock.com: 45 and front cover
© Charly Kurz / Laif / Contrasto: 90–91
© Eric Lafforgue / Gamma-Rapho via Getty Images: 103
© Martin Lyle / Medavia.co.uk: 151–155
© Véronique Mergaux: 49–55 and back cover (l.)
© Mondadori Portfolio / Giuseppe Pino: 165–167
© Carlo Morucchio / Robertharding / Corbis: 42–43
© Fabio Motta / dpa / Corbis: 83–85
© Yuriko Nakao / Getty Images: 77, 80–81
© Newfotosud Franco Romano / Olycom: 98–101
© Pietro Paolini / TerraProject / Contrasto: 97
© Klaus Pichler / Anzenberger: 112–113
© Ron Pollard Englewood, Colorado: 71–75
© Leo Ramirez / AFP / Getty Images: 123, 126–127
© Reuters / David Gray / Contrasto: 24–25
© Reuters / Siphiwe Sibeko / Contrasto: 35
© Reuters / STR New / Contrasto: 104–105
© Reuters / Bobby Yip / Contrasto: 106–107
© Reza / Getty Images: 92–93
© Darmon Richter / The Bohemian Blog: 169–175
© The Asahi Shimbun via Getty Images: 78–79
© Theo Volpatti / Contrasto: 147–149
© Xinhua / eyevine / Contrasto: 36–37
© Alexander Zaitsev: 115–121

The publisher is at the disposal of all copyright holders for any
queries about unidentified iconographic sources.

Alessandro Biamonti is an architect and professor in the Department of Design at the Politecnico di Milano, where he has coordinated the Research Team of the Lab.I.R.Int (Laboratory of Innovation and Research on Interiors) since 2005. He has also curated several editions of the Milano Design PhD Festival. Through his teaching and profession, Biamonti has explored the anthropological dimension of design for years, and presented his approach to an international public at lectures and conferences.

To Rino – he knows why …

ALESSANDRO BIAMONTI

ARCHIFLOP

A guide to the most spectacular failures in the history
of modern and contemporary architecture

niggli

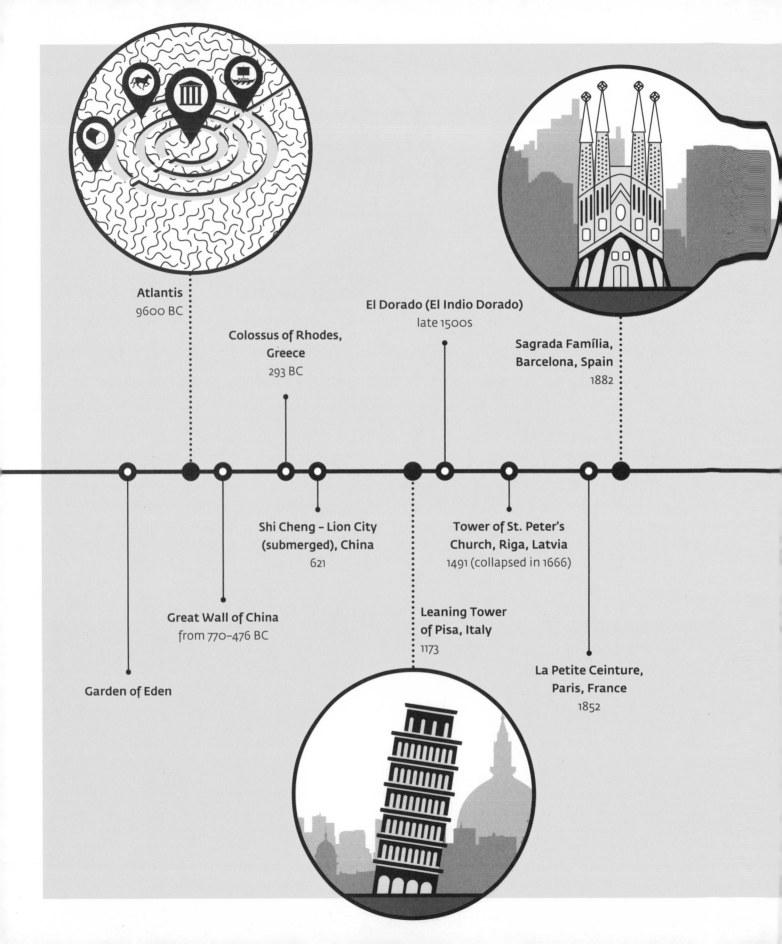

Atlantis
9600 BC

Colossus of Rhodes, Greece
293 BC

El Dorado (El Indio Dorado)
late 1500s

Sagrada Família, Barcelona, Spain
1882

Shi Cheng – Lion City (submerged), China
621

Tower of St. Peter's Church, Riga, Latvia
1491 (collapsed in 1666)

Great Wall of China
from 770–476 BC

Leaning Tower of Pisa, Italy
1173

La Petite Ceinture, Paris, France
1852

Garden of Eden